ADVANCE PRAISE

"I have reviewed dozens of leadership books throughout my professional career and Ted Kulawiak's *21 Lessons Learned in Leadership* stands out as a smart, sincere, and thoughtful read. I highly recommend new and seasoned leaders read as all 21 lessons provide sound advice with practical, easy to follow stories associated with each lesson. The insights shared can help elevate a leader's behavior, actions, and performance. I would consider this a must-read for any leader both formal and informal, looking to strengthen their skills, communication, and overall results."

Elise Awwad, COO, Higher Education Industry

"Ted's approach to writing as well as his views on leadership are practical, illustrative, thoughtful and, above all else, insightful. *21 Lessons Learned in Leadership* contains invaluable, application-oriented information for all who previously led, as well as current and aspiring leaders. Ted's book contains a lifetime worth of important lessons learned in sales, management and leadership."

Rick Borowiak, Director, Training

"Ted captures experiences in life lessons that are truly wonderful from which to learn. These are thoughtful stories that can be passed on to all leaders at any stage in their career. This is a leadership book to be consumed and shared!"
Wayne Brantley, President, 360 Training Solutions

"Too often the term leadership is considered a buzzword. In *21 Lessons Learned in Leadership* Ted provides interesting and compelling real-life examples of true leadership that provide substance to the term. His lessons learned remind me of both superior and poor leadership situations I've experienced through my career, and why I've always tried to exhibit true leadership-by-example for my teams."
Bill Geary, CFO

"The stories contained in *21 Lessons Learned in Leadership* will inspire anyone to be a better leader and human being – and if the importance of the messages about humility, respect, teamwork, and empowerment aren't crystal clear, then leadership shouldn't be a part of your future."
Linda Hoopes PhD, VP, Higher Education Industry

"*21 Lessons Learned in Leadership* is not just another book on leadership. Ted takes a more genuine approach by providing a compilation of short lessons, incorporating his first-hand life experiences, and acknowledging his personal influencers along the way. He does a wonderful job showcasing the ingredients needed for an effective leader. I often paused, and self-related during my read. This book is an easy read, relatable with a bit of personality and a twist of humor."

Theresa Kennedy, The Coca-Cola Company

"I have read many books on leadership but this one is exceptional. Ted brings the book life with relatable well-known people throughout history and their experiences. He then breaks down the key elements needed to find success in any situation. This book makes leadership more attainable for all through great lessons which are easy to implement."

Bethany Moran, VP, Higher Education Industry

"*21 Lessons Learned in Leadership* is not your run of the mill dry primer on how to be an outstanding leader. I found the real-life stories of people using these principles combined with Ted's wisdom and experiences make for an engaging and valuable read. The Leadership in Action section at the end of every chapter targets each skill explicated with insight and humor. This book can be one's go-to reference again and again for business …and for life."

Joyce Renneke, CTA Certified Life Coach

"Ted offers *21 Lessons Learned in Leadership* with real life examples from successful leaders that we get to know and wish to emulate. New leaders will find this book provides vision and great advice to set you on your own path to success. Seasoned leaders will recognize easily identifiable experiences. Most likely you will, as I did, have the added pleasure of new ideas that build on your past success. Enjoy!"

Cheryl Renner Whitney, Learning & Development Leader

Allison,

21 LESSONS LEARNED
IN LEADERSHIP

"TO LEAD OTHERS is BOTH
AN HONOR AND A PRIVILEGE.
TO LEAD ADMIRABLY
is A BLESSING." T.K.

#LiveTOLEAD!

21 LESSONS LEARNED IN LEADERSHIP

TED KULAWIAK

Charleston, SC
www.PalmettoPublishing.com

21 Lessons Learned in Leadership
Copyright © 2021 by Ted Kulawiak
All rights reserved

First Edition

Printed in the United States

Paperback ISBN: 978-1-63837-701-6

DEDICATION

This book is dedicated to those who yearn to lead, those who lead admirably, and those who led with lasting positive impact.

To the leaders that influenced me in my business career as they provided sound guidance, support, and encouragement, but especially to those who also provided constructive feedback as needed. I appreciated your candor and direction, but most importantly I appreciated your actions, which spoke volumes of your inherent leadership skills.

My coworkers, direct reports, and peers in business throughout my career, thank you for the opportunity to learn from you, lead with you, and journey together. We had some rocky terrain to navigate at times, and we also had plenty of laughs, successes, and accomplishments. We built lasting friendships for which I am grateful.

To those family, friends, and business associates listed in the acknowledgments section, thank you for your input and for sharing numerous leadership-in-action examples. Your participation was invaluable.

Robin, thirty-one years and counting.

CONTENTS

Foreword   xiii

Lesson #1: Leadership in Action is Leadership Defined   1

Lesson #2: Your Vision, Your Values, Your Culture   8

Lesson #3: Be a Great Human Being   24

Lesson #4: Show Up   34

Lesson #5: Get Ahead of the Curve   46

Lesson #6: Leadership and Trust   61

Lesson #7: The Ladder Goes Both Ways   73

Lesson #8: There Is No Power If There Is No Resistance   82

Lesson #9: Leadership and Conflict   93

Lesson #10: Be Determined, Be Influential   104

Lesson #11: Leadership and Ethics   116

Lesson #12: Entrepreneurial Leadership   129

Lesson #13: I Have Your Back   142

Lesson #14: Be a Great Teammate   150

Lesson #15: Leadership and Coaching with Commitment   162

Lesson #16: Communicate with Purpose   176

Lesson #17: Leadership and Community   186

Lesson #18: Leadership and Capacity   197

Lesson #19: Serve to Inspire   207

Lesson #20: Get Involved and Act   216

Lesson #21: On the Way to Becoming a Great Leader,

Be a Great Manager as Well   226

Bonus Lesson Learned   237

Acknowledgments   239

About Ted Kulawiak   240

About David Pauldine   242

FOREWORD

By David Pauldine

Leadership is like beauty; it is hard to define, but
you know it when you see it. Leadership is not doing
things right; it's more doing the right thing.
—Warren Bennis

You are about to read a book about leadership. When Ted asked me to write this foreword, I asked him what he wanted to accomplish with this, his second book. I listened as he told me his motivation was to bring forth a range of leadership content uniquely "teed up" by a selection of professionals with whom Ted had interacted over his career. In short, he wanted this book on leadership to be a "work of many hands." He told me he wanted the book to be written in a practical, pragmatic way with an emphasis on illustrations, stories, best practices, and meaningful experiences, all of which would increase reader interest while getting the messages across. Ted then cut me loose with the challenge to find a message that would be fitting for the foreword of this book.

I'd like to get started by introducing the following formula: theory + application = knowledge. This formula makes the case that the best way to learn is to combine the *theory* often obtained from a book or classroom with the *application* of that theory in the real world, such as on the job. Years ago I worked in a technical school. Faculty would deliver a classroom lecture for an hour or so, then tell the students to take a break and afterward show up in the tech lab for a two-hour hands-on session. In those two hours, the students would apply what they had learned in the classroom session by working directly with the equipment. This mix of theory and application maximized learning. So now let's talk about theory and application in the context of leadership.

When in grad school, I chose a program solely focused on leadership. At the time we were exposed to the writings of several of the gurus of leadership—Warren Bennis, Noel Tichy, Daniel Katz and Robert Khan, Abraham Zaleznik, Peter Senge, Max DePree, Edgar Schein, John Kotter, James Heskett, Burt Nanus, and others. As you'd expect, these icons had spent years researching the subject of leadership and had lots to say. Their writings most certainly touched on the essential components of leadership, including the role leadership plays in establishing mission, vision, and values. Moreover, they spoke to the topics of culture, ethics, strategic planning, high-performing work teams, talent acquisition, talent development, and business execution. I remember also a fair amount being written on the comparison of leadership and management. I bring this up to highlight the importance of theory in one's pursuit of knowledge about leadership. In listening to Ted describe his vision for this book, I am going to go out on a limb and say that this is not a book about leadership theory.

This is a book loaded with real-world *applications* for leadership. You will be exposed to numerous examples, stories, illustrations, anecdotes, and events that get to the heart of what leadership is all about. In this way you should find *21 Lessons Learned in Leadership* a quick read.

One last point. I've worked with many excellent leaders who probably could not tell you in clinical terms what effective leadership is but who would be quick to say, "I'll know it when I see it." I'm confident you'll "see it" in the chapters ahead. Similarly, we often say, "Don't just tell me; show me." That's what this book is about to do. You'll see that as you read on. Let's tee things up with an example.

Warren Bennis shared a story of a leadership event that took place in Iraq during the first Gulf War. There was a war correspondent working for a major media outlet that was covering the conflict. He was in his Baghdad hotel watching CNN when a breaking news story was being covered. It was taking place in the holy city of Najaf. This is an Iraqi town known for its mosques and religious gatherings. The US Army was marching through the heart of town. The locals were anxious about this and gathered around to watch the US troops. The crowd size grew as onlookers began to talk and question what was taking place. There was a fear that the US Army might do damage to the town or if nothing else, disrespect its holiness. The journalist could feel the tension while watching the events unfold on live television. He thought for certain a rock would be thrown, perhaps some pushing, and shoving would take place, and then God forbid, a shot would be fired. If that were to take place, the journalist feared the Iraq equivalent of Viet Nam's My Lai incident would ensue, and perhaps hundreds would be killed. Then, out of nowhere, one US soldier stepped in front of his brigade and took a knee. At the same time, he took his rifle and pointed its barrel to the ground. This was a nonverbal show of peace—signifying he meant no harm. The locals looked on with great interest. Then another soldier did the same, then another. One by one the members of the unit took a knee, pointing the nose of their rifles to the ground. The tension and anxiety of the crowd disappeared. No longer was there fear of an incident. The villagers, comfortable that this army of foreigners meant no harm, retreated back to their homes and shops. Not a shot was fired; no one was hurt.

Later this journalist shared that he was struck by the quick thinking of the US soldier who first took a knee and neutered his weapon. This was an extemporaneous act of leadership. What he did was likely not something one could read about in a book or even learn in a classroom. Yet his quick thinking was an act of leadership in the greatest of terms, and one that likely saved many lives. It would be hard for us to point to a leadership theory that addressed this act or to put a label on it. But, for certain, it was an act of leadership that fits into the category of "I'll know it when I see it."

On to *21 Lessons Learned in Leadership*. I have to believe you'll be better off having read what lies ahead.

LESSON #1: LEADERSHIP IN ACTION IS LEADERSHIP DEFINED

The ultimate measure of a man is not where he stands in moments of comfort, but where he stands at times of challenge and controversy.
—Dr. Martin Luther King Jr.

The assignment was daunting, the orders direct. *Hold the flank.* Lieutenant Colonel Joshua Lawrence Chamberlain, a former professor of language and rhetoric at Bowdoin College from the state of Maine, had been given the most important assignment he had ever received. At the battle of Gettysburg, July 1–4, 1863, during America's Civil War, as the leader of the Federal Army's Twentieth Maine troops, Chamberlain and his men were tasked with holding the line to the extreme left of the Federal's main body of troops. He and his men were dug in yet spread out on the part of the battlefield known as Little Round Top. To his advantage, Chamberlain held the higher ground as the terrain of Little Round Top proved a natural stronghold. In order for the Confederate troops to overcome Twentieth Maine's position, they would have to fight uphill. Measurably a daunting task as presented, but not an insurmountable one. Chamberlain was determined to hold the flank and positioned his men to take full advantage of the terrain, which provided natural cover in the form of trees and rocks along with its steep incline. As the Confederates would engage in the uphill battle, Chamberlain would instruct his men to hold their position, defend at all costs, and repel the attackers back down the hill.

Chamberlain was confident in his plan. *Hold the flank.*

He and the Twentieth Maine troops were ready to disrupt any Confederate aggression aimed at the Federal forces from the extreme left of the main body of Federal troops. However, Chamberlain also realized the gravity of the situation. If he and his men were unable to ward off the Confederate attack, the Federal Army would be exposed, attacked from the side and ultimately from behind. The flanking maneuver is designed to attack an opposition army at it least defensible point, and Chamberlain's Twentieth Maine soldiers were the focal point of that least defensible opposition.

Under the leadership of Colonel William C. Oates, the Confederate Fifteenth Regiment Alabama Infantry were given their own set of orders. *Attack and overcome the Federal left flank.* Their plan was to attack the Federal forces at their least defensible and most vulnerable point, force the Federal defenders off of Little Round Top, and ultimately engage the Federal main body of troops from the side and behind. Their goal and the results they hoped for were clear. While an uphill battle, victory could be accomplished. If successful, it would change the outcome of the war.

Oates believed that success in this endeavor would mean certain victory for the Confederate Army of Northern Virginia at Gettysburg and would open the path for a march to take Washington, DC. He and his men were determined to overcome Chamberlain's tactical advantage through a series of assaults designed to overwhelm the Federal firepower and position. Oates knew that he could outgun and outman the Federal troops despite their positioning. He would *attack and overcome the Federal left flank*. The Federals would not be able to withstand a relentless, continuous series of assaults, and thereby the Confederate Fifteenth Regiment Alabama would be successful in this battle.

Oates was confident in his plan. *Attack and overcome the Federal left flank*.

On the second day of the Gettysburg battle, July 2, 1863, Oates launched his plan. Wave after wave of Confederate soldiers braved the difficult terrain and made their way up Little Round Top. Relentless in their efforts, the Confederates displayed a fierce aggression in meeting the uphill challenge. They fought with intensity and determination to oust the Federal defenders.

Yet each time they advanced, they were met with an equally fierce and determined group of Federal soldiers, steadfast in protecting their position. The battle was waged throughout the day, with both sides suffering heavy casualties. Yet neither side would retreat or relinquish their effort. To add to the drama, the Federal soldiers were running short on ammunition. Maybe Oates had been right. If he could outgun and outman the Federals, the Confederates would gain Little Round Top and win the battle.

What Oates did not forecast and calculate correctly, however, was the leadership skill of his opponent, the college professor turned soldier Joshua Lawrence Chamberlain. As he was faced with having little to no ammunition, the logical directive for Chamberlain would have been to fall back, retreat, and get to a position of fortitude to reinforce his troops. In doing so, however, while strengthening his troop's position, he would be giving up Little Round Top. He would be allowing the Confederates to enact their strategy to push his men off of the landscape, which held the key to battle victory or defeat.

His next decision proved to be the turning point in the day's battle.

Rather than withdraw his troops to regroup to safer ground and thereby forfeit a prime piece of battle real estate, Chamberlain determined his best plan of action for the sake of the main Federal Army was to repel the Confederates from Little Round Top and thereby ordered an attack on the Confederates, a bayonet attack no less. His Twentieth Maine soldiers, exhausted from a day's fighting with the enemy and many without ammunition, were going to run down the hill directly into their oncoming opponents. They would do this in a series of single-line waves, like a hinge on a door swinging open and shut. As the first wave went down the hill, the second wave would follow and swing into the enemy, bayonets extended, placing life and limb for both attacker and defender at highest risk. Hand-to-hand combat.

Hold the flank.

As brutal as that sounds—and one can only imagine the horror of the scenario—Chamberlain gave the order, and the Twentieth Maine troops engaged the Confederates with a strategic leadership tactic Oates had not anticipated. He was now the defender under extreme attack from the Federal soldiers. The surprise maneuver proved Chamberlain's decision-making to be correct as the Twentieth Maine was successful in clearing the Confederates from advancing on Little Round Top and thereby was successful in following through on their orders to *hold the flank.*

Chamberlain's quick and critical thinking as the leader of the Twentieth Maine, under extreme pressure, is not only to be admired but also a lesson through which to learn. Leadership is not passive, theoretical, or cavalier. True leadership is founded in action-oriented opportunities. It is focused, proactive, influential, and strategic, yet it is the leader's actions, especially in crisis, that impact the results.

There is no leadership without action.

Everything in a plan designed to move a business forward is just a plan. It is nothing without the subsequent action of the owner/leader to engage and properly execute the plan. Having a strategy is like having good intentions. Proper execution of the strategy delivers results.

True leadership is demonstrated by influential actions. In a time of crisis, that particular moment will reveal everything one needs to know about the leader. In Chamberlain's situation, his bold and courageous decision demonstrated superior recognition and leadership in action. Although with a level of high risk, he determined forward aggression to be his best course of action, his best option. His decisive action was to throw away the textbook military training that called for him and his men to fall back, retreat, and get to safer ground. I can only imagine how serious he was in making his decision to attack instead of retreat. And he did so in a short amount of time under extremely difficult conditions.

Exemplary leadership is founded in action and deemed a success or failure through the measurable results of those actions.

In this book you will find content consistently focused on leaders who acted to define their leadership skill set rather than on textbook theories or philosophies. The examples provided are true-to-life situations, opinions, thoughts, actions, and stories that will be easy to relate to your own situation. Some examples are from my own experiences, yet the majority are from renowned business leaders, friends, family members, and associates.

All lessons learned offer a significant leadership characteristic illustrated in an actionable scenario. I believe you will find this book to be an easy read yet will also find it to have depth in knowledge and provide practical applications to both your professional and personal life.

Also, there's a little bit of humor at the end of each lesson designed to lighten the load of this serious topic.

Enjoy.

Courage: Mental, physical, social, emotional, intellectual, spiritual, or moral strength to venture, persevere, and withstand danger, fear, or difficulty.

Leadership in Action: As a leader of the sales and revenue generating team, there is nothing that better demonstrates courage than being called on to explain to the board of directors a shortfall to expectations in quarterly sales results. There is no place to hide, nowhere to run.

Telling it like it is takes courage, and bluffing is not an option.

LESSON #2: YOUR VISION, YOUR VALUES, YOUR CULTURE

Customers will never love a company
until the employees love it first.
—Simon Sinek

Old-school thinking indoctrinates business owners with the philosophy that the "customer is always right." Regardless of the situation and the circumstances, the customer dictates the success of the business. And of course without customers there is no business. Traditionalists format their approach to day-to-day business operations with a foundation that is customer-centric, customer-focused, customer-oriented. This direction is carried as the flag and written about in the mission of the organization, demonstrated in the core values, and expressed as the leader's vision and priority. Customers will be treated with the ultimate respect, courtesy, accommodation, and service so as to place their best interests above any and all else that matters. In most instances it is the customer that dictates the success of the business. Perhaps deservedly so, as the customers are the business.

While it is certainly admirable to place emphasis on customer satisfaction, there are many times and circumstances I have personally witnessed whereby the customer was not right. In fact, the customer was flat-out wrong and was merely trying to place themselves in a position of opportunity, to take advantage of the situation for their own personal gain. No level of customer satisfaction would be absolutely acceptable to the customer without it being at the ultimate expense of the business. After all, over the course of years, the customer was indoctrinated much the same way as the business owner. The customer is in charge of transactions and demands to be treated with utmost appreciation for their business. They recognize their advantage and leverage their buying capacity to its maximum. In their eyes, they are always right.

Unfortunately for the old-school line of thinking, overemphasis on the customer and their needs allows for a shortsighted approach to the reality of business operations. While the customers may be happy to a certain extent, their transactional "me first" attitude certainly provides a challenge to employees faced with carrying out unrealistic demands. This disconnect creates a rift between what old-school leadership desires and what modern employees seek in an organization.

Employees, just like customers, want to be happy, respected, empowered, and appreciated for their efforts to make the organization successful. So much so that customers are no longer considered to be the foundation of a blossoming organization. Highly engaged employees, and their enthusiastic approach to conducting business, have taken the lead. For without exemplary employees to take care of customers, there will be no customers, or at least a diminished number of customers, and definitely fewer repeat customers.

Thus the current foundational approach to organizational leadership is based in finding balance between treating employees as well as, if not better than, customers are treated. The thinking is that employees who are treated well will appreciate their surroundings and their opportunities, love their jobs, and will reflect that satisfaction in their customer interactions. Provided those employees are trained, competent, and willing to do their jobs as expected, the business should at least have a good starting point to be successful. Totally makes sense, doesn't it? Is this a revolutionary approach to business best practices?

Hardly. The late great former CEO of Southwest Airlines Herb Kelleher implemented this strategic vision years ago in building Southwest to be one of the most successful business operations in the world. His belief was that employees should be treated like customers, and in so doing, their satisfaction in their jobs would in turn be reflected in their treatment of customers. This internal focus would inspire the Southwest employees to be their best, and ultimately their actions would lead to customer satisfaction and repeat business. By taking care of his own "family," Herb Kelleher instituted a disruptive approach to traditional business thinking.

And it worked, as Southwest is celebrating its fifty-fourth year in business and throughout that time has received numerous employee and customer satisfaction awards, while turning a profit. The Southwest vision statement is in accordance with the company's intent: "To become the world's most loved, most flown, and most profitable airline." Southwest's core values are centered around employees who work hard, treat others with respect, and have fun in their daily efforts. They focus internally to drive external satisfaction.

Numerous organizations are taking this approach to building out their culture to reflect employee satisfaction as a prime motivator of business success. Organization's such as Salesforce, Workday, PayPal, and HubSpot regularly publish and promote their employee satisfaction surveys as a principle for establishing and continuing emphasis on their employee's well-being and as a method to attract future employees. Their emphasis on providing the employee a unique and awesome work experience via exceptional perks such as in-house daycare, salary equality, flexible work hours, and remote work options, to name a few, makes these organizations destination workplaces. It doesn't hurt that these organizations have a robust product and platform with high consumer demand, yet the leaders in these operations realize they are accountable for supporting a culture that meets the business objectives and balances the best interests of the employee's personal well-being. They have done it successfully and are to be commended for their commitment to this generation of employees' expectations.

If you believe that a company's culture is founded in a company's values, based on its mission, and realized through its vision, then you are very likely to also believe leadership in the company has a responsibility to enact the vision, values, and mission in everyday business dealings. And not just to enact but also engage and actually live the vision, values, and mission. Leadership has a responsibility to establish, implement, and live up to these principles that are the organization's forward-facing mantra.

In that regard I was happy to engage several of my former colleagues to get their input on leadership as it relates to creating vision, values, and mission statements for their respective organizations. But more importantly I had the opportunity to gauge their thoughts about the importance of being a leader in action when it comes to owning these principles, specifically with the intent to understand how effective leaders hold themselves and their peers accountable to living the "talk."

One of my former colleagues is a gentleman named Matt Kinnich.

Matt is the CEO of FMT Solutions, an organization founded by retirement education veterans whose mission is to help fiduciary advisers improve their clients' lives through financial education. FMT Solutions believes that a fiduciary adviser has a responsibility to always act in their clients' best interests. The best way to help a client make good financial decisions is to educate them. FMT Solutions is selective in whom they allow to become licensed instructors: in order to qualify, prospective instructors must have sufficient industry licensing and credentials and agree to not market any financial products during their class.

Matt told me about the exercise his organization went through, which were much like other organization's efforts to build out FMT's vision, values, and mission. Over the course of several weeks, cross-functional team members from various levels came together and worked in pods addressing questions regarding the organization's platform. The exercise was designed to determine "who we are as a company," "how we act," and most importantly "how we behave with others." The "others" in this case included coworkers, customers, suppliers, and those who had regular interactions with FMT.

Critical to the process was the acceptance by senior leadership that they alone would not dictate the results. Senior leaders shared equal roles with FMT Solutions coworkers who had equal voice in sharing their thoughts about what the vision, values, and mission should look like when completed. All were empowered. All were able to participate. All had an equal say-so in the creation of the key platforms. And all took accountability and responsibility for sharing the outcomes of the exercise within the organization.

As Matt outlined the process for the vision, values, and mission initiative, he also told me about what he considers to be the three essential aspects of effective leadership in his effort to build a culture that allows coworkers to demonstrate leadership behaviors. His emphasis on the premise that leadership is not a title but more so an action is grounded in these three key characteristics.

In order to be effective a leader must:

- **Demonstrate authenticity**—be who you are, be authentic, be real, be the person who lives up to the organization's expectations daily.
- **Be collaborative**—take an approach that encourages empowerment, which allows others to make decisions, share best practices, develop, and grow as an organization with a common commitment to desired results
- **Be direct and honest**—deal with problems in a straightforward manner, and always take the ethical approach in all situations.

Matt believes that in order to be effective, a leader must create an environment that allows employees the freedom to work with autonomy, which allows them to make decisions at their own appropriate level of engagement. This autonomy sets the tone for improved performance and improved productivity and drives employee engagement and satisfaction. It is this culture that permeates the organization, whereby the customer experience is standardized. Regardless of which department in the organization the customer contacts, they will receive the same high level of exceptional service in line with FMT Solution's commitment to its employees to take care of its customers.

In order to encourage a culture of commitment, Matt instituted town hall meetings, held on a monthly basis, which later became online weekly town hall sessions. While the model of keeping employees in tune and engaged via town halls didn't change, the velocity and volume increased as an example of leadership in action, as well as recognition of the importance of keeping in touch during remote work restrictions. These town hall meeting are the glue that keeps the organization connected, and perhaps while not unique, as other organizations provide a similar communications platform, the FMT Solutions town hall is well appreciated for the opportunity it provides to share camaraderie, fun, a little trivia, and even some collaborative business discussion.

My final question to Matt concerned his personal mentors, those he admired and from whom he had learned. I wanted to know what people had done to guide his career and to make a positive impression on his leadership style. Matt summarized his answer into two key qualities that all of his mentors have in common.

They are consummate professionals in all of their daily activities and interactions.

They are great human beings who exemplify the importance of treating others with the same level of respect as they would like to be treated with.

It doesn't get much clearer than that. Being professional and a being a great human to others are foundational qualities of exemplary leaders.

Another person whom I have great respect for and had the pleasure of speaking with recently is a gentleman named Steve Riehs.

Steve is a leader, friend, mentor, and a person I got to know during his time as the group president of medical, professional, and online education for Adtalem Global Education. In this capacity at Adtalem, Steve was the leader who grew the online division to become the fifth largest online university in the United States. During this time he launched Chamberlain College of Nursing online programs, which became the market leader. He led the effort to acquire eight Brazilian universities, expanded the Becker CPA prep division, and improved performance of the international medical division (Ross Medical School, Ross Veterinarian School).

Based on his experience and level of responsibility, Steve is the type of person who takes a direct, heads on personal approach to defining what leadership in action looks like. His position on leadership core values come as no surprise to me, as I had worked with Steve for several years.

In Steve's eyes, in order to be effective, a leader must have a commitment to personal core values in these areas:

- **Integrity**—the leader must operate with the highest level of honesty and sense of purpose in doing the right thing
- **Compliance**—the minimum required table stakes in order to get in the game; being compliant with the organization's rules are a given and complement the leader's sense of integrity
- **Commitment**—the leader must demonstrate a personal passion for living the organization core values by being a role model of engagement

Critical to having a personal set of core values is the leader's dedication to building a culture that defines how coworkers treat each other and how the company as a whole treats its customers. In direct support of both personal and organizational core values, the leader must be willing to hire, discipline, and, if needed, fire people based on their individual commitment to and demonstration of those core values. Live up to expectations as defined in the core values, and things will be fine. Break the rules, and the consequences will speak for themselves. The commitment to core values is essential to exemplary leadership.

By the same token, poor leadership turns a blind eye to those performers who deliver results at an exceptional level but who are challenged to guide themselves and live their organizational life within the boundaries of the defined core values. Thereby those poor leaders effectively disregard their commitment to doing the right things, working with integrity and honesty, and will not enforce the rules for top performers. Working in highly regulated environments where there is increased scrutiny and optics are consistently under the microscope, the poor leader risks career and reputation by ignoring coworkers who fail to live up to the core values. The leader's inaction is in itself an action that says they don't care.

Leaders need to define what winning looks like and more importantly what winning by operating with complete integrity looks like. Coworkers are aware of their responsibility to operate within company rules, and their performance is measured in this regard. The scorekeeping aspect of leadership defines how well employees have succeeded in their commitment to deliver results in an ethical manner. In communicating this directive to the organization, the leader must be able to deliver the message in a manner to which all coworkers can relate. If values create culture and culture defines whether a customer will buy from the company, then employees must understand the significance of living up to the values and be able to identify with this importance on a daily basis. Therefore it is the leader's responsibility to ensure the message is delivered in terms that everyone understands.

My final question to Steve concerned his personal mentors. Steve identified two key learnings that all of his mentors have in common.

People are always watching the leader; they have significant opportunity to provide feedback and will do so without fail at times when the leader's commitment to integrity is in question.

Truly effective leaders have a good heart; they understand people and are experts at balancing their business and relationship agenda.

Someone once told me that as a person rises in responsibility in an organization, the size of the target on that person's back becomes larger with each level upgrade. People are always watching to see if the leader will err and are prompt to point out those errors. It is best to own up to mistakes in judgment, yet it is even better to operate with complete integrity at all times.

I also had the pleasure of speaking with Kirk Paille, who is the vice president of partnerships at AVENU Learning. I like to think I had a small bit of influence on Kirk's career development as we worked together years ago, but it's more likely that Kirk earned his career progression via hard work, dedication, and his continuous personal development.

As a leading global provider of educational services, AVENU works with universities and other educational providers to extend boundaries and reimagine the transnational learner. Kirk is responsible for managing all client university relationships and managing a team of cross-functional managers to achieve revenue expectations for client partners. In addition, Kirk works closely with AVENU partners to launch new programs and enhance processes to provide an outstanding student experience.

In my discussion with Kirk, I asked him to define what he believes to be the foundation of leadership. He summed it up in one simple word—trust. In order to be a truly effective leader, the leader must earn trust and demonstrate the same with the associates. Kirk summed up his approach to gaining trust as a two-way street between leader and coworker, with these key elements at the core of the relationship:

- **Be genuine**—relate to others in a way that allows them to know you understand who they are; be real. If you speak from the heart, people will have a much better opinion of who you are. If you try to be someone you are not, others will sense your false approach and will easily turn away from you. Stay true to who you are, and others will appreciate you from that standpoint. They may not like you, but at least they will appreciate you!

- **Communicate**—regularly address the team, spend time with them, tell them what's going on, and most importantly, ask for their input. Leading is a visible undertaking and one that provides opportunity to engage coworkers. Take advantage of every opportunity to engage your coworkers in meaningful conversation. Be respectful, take the time to listen, and question with the intent to learn.

- **Be accountable**—this is also a two-way street, yet it is important for the leader to set the tone for being responsible and owning up to mistakes. There is a mutual level of respect granted when the leader accepts being accountable and expects the same in return from coworkers. There is no place for finger-pointing or placing blame.

Kirk also mentioned that part of the leader's responsibility to drive the organization's culture is the ability to influence others in a positive meaningful manner—and not just to get things done, but more so for the purpose of generating new ideas and providing an opportunity for others to feel comfortable in their willingness to participate.

A passionate leader skilled in the art of influence can engage others to share the same passion.

An influential leader creates a culture of engagement based on the comfort level of others and their willingness to provide meaningful input.

It is evident from my discussions with these three leaders that at the core of vision, values, and mission is the leader's understanding of people and ability to build a culture that supports an open, empowered relationship through this understanding. Critical to this concept is identifying what behaviors and beliefs should be valued by the organization and ensuring all employees understand the importance of living up to those values.

Therefore it is the leader who influences the vision, values, and mission throughout the organization. It is the leader in action who owns the vision and values and sets the tone for the organization's culture. This is an employee expectation. Most importantly this is a requirement of an organization that desires to be employee-centric, employee-focused, and employee-oriented to drive customer satisfaction. The exemplary leader drives a thriving internal culture with engaged employees who therefore love the organization for how they are respected, treated, empowered, and appreciated. Leadership commitment to employees in this manner is reciprocated via the employee's passionate commitment to the customer. That commitment to the customer is the key leadership influential. For without employees there can be no customers. And without customers there can be no business.

> **Influence:** The power or capacity to cause an effect in indirect or intangible ways, to affect or alter by indirect or intangible means.

> **Leadership in Action:** Effective and impactful leaders have an inherent ability and develop the capacity to influence others to carry out their requests without having to directly order their con-

stituents to do so. The followers are willing to carry out their assignments at the bequest of the leader.

I've experienced being the person of influence as well as the person being influenced. Most recently this occurred with my four-year-old grandson, who interpreted my "sharing is healthy" influence lesson with the response "Papa, I know you want to share a chocolate with me." Of course he is right, and of course he wins the discussion.

LESSON #3: BE A GREAT HUMAN BEING

Be the reason someone smiles. Be the reason someone feels loved and believes in the goodness of people.
—Roy T. Bennett

It is easy to get caught up in the pursuit of success. Or at least in what we are led to believe is success. We are consistently bombarded with an overwhelming emphasis on making a lot of money, beating the competition, gaining material luxuries, and living the so-called dream. This one-sided pressure messaging can corrupt a business leader caught up in the obligation to be the organization's strategist for monetary growth while downplaying the importance of this person also being the organization's chief humanistic visionary. The definition of success is different for everyone as it is a personalized approach to what makes an individual happy. Yet there is no doubt leaders come under intense scrutiny to balance the pursuit of business profit and the promotion of a people-first culture. After all, if you don't have great people, you don't have a great business.

Now some of you reading that prior sentence may be thinking, *If you're not focused on your business, your customers, and in making a profit, you don't have a business* (see lesson #2). People will feel much better about their jobs when they have jobs. So it should be business first, people second. After all, if you don't have a great business, you don't have a need for great people.

Six of one, half dozen of the other?

I don't think so. I believe the two schools of thought are equally intertwined, complex, and essential to any business' success. But I believe results through people will always take precedent in my leadership thinking. Maybe that's why so late in my career I decided to go it alone and be my own boss. At least I know who to blame if things go south.

When people feel their work is appreciated, are able to voice their opinion without fear of retaliation, and work in a culture where work is challenging yet enjoyable, creating an atmosphere for productivity is much more likely to occur. The leader of a small team, large department, or entire organization is the person accountable for establishing the culture that delivers that company atmosphere, vibe, buzz, and feeling. The leader owns the culture.

I believe positive results achieved are an outcome of the direct proportion between the skill and ability of a satisfied, happy employee and the willingness of that employee to put forth the required effort. Barring unforeseen circumstances or market differentials, empowering able and willing employees normally translates to positive results for the organization.

Yet establishing an environment that supports the premise of empowering able and willing employees is only part of the equation. Also critical to success are the actions of the leader to support that positive environment and ultimately support the organization's people.

> *To be successful in leadership, provide support for people in the organization during the most difficult of circumstances. Be a human being first.*

With that thought in mind, my friend Terry McDougall submitted a story to me for this book that reinforced my belief regarding successful leaders whose actions demonstrate a complete understanding of this leadership principle.

Terry is the owner of her own executive coaching firm, Terry B. McDougall Coaching, and best-selling author of *Winning the Game of Work: Career Happiness and Success on Your Own Terms*. I was thrilled that she answered my request to submit an exemplary leadership case. Based on Terry's background in a high-profile marketing career, I knew she would submit a legitimate real-life scenario on which I could build a lesson learned. I expected it was going to be a leadership example based on the relationship between marketing and sales, her expertise and mine. Or maybe it would be an example from her coaching business whereby she guided an executive to improved personal growth.

What I received was not anticipated, but certainly made an impression.

Terry told me a story about an experience that occurred early in her marketing career in the financial services industry. She was pregnant with her third and last child. One of her direct reports was a young lady—we will call her Jenna—who was pregnant with her first child. Jenna was going to have a baby girl. Prior to Jenna starting maternity leave, Terry took Jenna to lunch on the Friday of her last week in the office to celebrate the big occasion. As you could imagine, the feelings of excitement and anticipation were a major focus during this lunch. The next time Terry and Jenna would see each other, Jenna would be a mom with a newborn.

Only it didn't turn out that way.

On the following Monday, Jenna called Terry at the office. Terry was so excited, wanting to hear all the details about the birth of Jenna's girl. "What is her name? How much did she weigh? How long did she measure?" Terry gushed with questions.

The voice on the other end of the phone was muted, not from exhaustion but from shock. Jenna told Terry that her daughter was stillborn.

The pain of those words were excruciating for Terry. Being at a loss for words at that time was an understatement. Terry was devastated. She felt guilty for her own pregnancy. She felt sorrow for Jenna. She felt pain and hurt. She felt anger at another one of life's unexpected tragedies. A full gamut of emotions ran through her as she struggled to compose herself and her thoughts and determine what she possibly could say to Jenna at this time to express her sympathy. Regaining herself after expressing her sorrow to Jenna, Terry knew she was faced with a monumental challenge. *How and what am I going to do to support Jenna?* was Terry's next thought.

After telling her coworkers of Jenna's tragic experience, Terry immediately went into action to answer her own question. She reached out to a friend who herself had lost a baby seven months into pregnancy. Terry told her friend the horrible news. Much to Terry's relief, in answer to the question "What should I do?" the friend insisted they drop everything and go to see Jenna in the hospital. It was the right thing to do. Go to the hospital, support Jenna and her husband. Be there for them at this tragic time.

Upon her arrival at Jenna's hospital room, Terry and her friend were greeted by Jenna's husband and her mother. Jenna's daughter, dressed in an adorable onesie, was also there in Jenna's arms. The tears flowed. Terry had not anticipated she would get to meet Jenna's daughter. She felt honored to be one of only a handful of people who would actually get the opportunity to meet Jenna's daughter. Other than having slightly darker lips, Jenna's baby looked like a perfect newborn, sleeping soundly in her mother's arms. She was beautiful. While one of the most powerful and touching moments in Terry's life, it was also one of the saddest things she had ever experienced. The tears flowed again.

As the months passed and Jenna recuperated both mentally and physically during her maternity leave, Terry learned the doctors had never provided Jenna with a definitive answer as to what had led to her daughter's death. It remained an unsolved mystery, with unanswered questions that Jenna would live with for the rest of her life. And within a few days, Jenna would be coming back to work. Terry knew she had to be mentally prepared for anything, yet facing Jenna would be difficult at best.

When Jenna returned to work, it was evident her mind wasn't in the game. While willing to get back into the work routine, she was struggling under the weight of her grief, which was affecting her ability to do her job. The tragedy was still fresh in her mind, and the grief she carried was visually evident. Terry described Jenna as a wounded doe. You could see the pain in her eyes. To make matters worse, Jenna returned at a remarkably busy time for the organization. They were the title sponsor of a Professional Golf Association (PGA) tour event and would be entertaining major clients in just a few short months. Terry and her team were responsible for a myriad of tasks leading up to and including the event and required maximum effort from all teammates, including Jenna, every day in order to meet the workload.

The business challenge itself presented Terry with a huge undertaking, but complicate that with Jenna's situation and the task at hand might have overwhelmed a lesser person. But not Terry.

She recognized her responsibility as a manager of task completion but also, more importantly, a leader of people support. Others in similar circumstances may have shied away from Jenna or pawned her off on human resources people or just flat-out ignored her. Others may have chosen to leave Jenna alone with a philosophy that she would be better off on her own—let her get back to work on her own terms, at her own pace. And while there is truth is the last statement regarding acceptance and pace of work, Terry knew she would be there for Jenna every day. Every day. Every. Single. Day.

This meant every morning when Jenna came to work, Terry would take the first part of the morning to meet with her. Terry would do a check-in support meeting with Jenna. Not a meeting to discuss details of the upcoming golf tournament, but a meeting focused solely on Jenna's frame of mind. "How's it going? How are you feeling? What do you need from me? How are you doing?" *It's all about Jenna, as it should be,* was Terry's thought. Other managers or leaders would not have directed so much attention to this one-on-one hand-holding personal approach. But not Terry. She made the consistent effort to be there for Jenna every day, and gradually Jenna turned the corner from being a seriously grief-stricken person and returned to being a valuable member of Terry's team.

The event went with off without a hitch, and Jenna contributed to its success, much to the admiration of Terry and her teammates. Jenna proved to be resilient in her effort to overcome the worst possible loss imaginable, and Terry was proud she had had a direct influence on Jenna's ability to impact a positive outcome.

In this gratifying moment, Terry learned the most valuable lesson of all in management and continues to carry that with her throughout her leadership career. It wasn't so much that Terry proved to be a good boss. *She proved to be a great human being.* Taking the time and making the extra effort to look out for another person, to show compassion, to care for another human being, and ensure that person's best interests were being met represented the pinnacle of Terry's experience. She transcended management/leadership achievements to attain a full understanding of success as taking a humanistic approach to others, not just when they are down, but at all times.

As mentioned previously, success is measured in an individual's personal definition of importance relative to their own intents. Yet too often success is defined in tangible items like wealth, trophies, cars, houses, and recognition. Those items may provide stimulus for motivation and represent the rewards of effort, but they do not justify the intent of leadership in action.

A true measure of success in leadership and leadership in action comes in an intangible emotional approach to the responsibility. It is best measured in response to crisis and support of those people deeply involved in that crisis. A leader reaches a different level of success when she realizes all those tangible items depend on the effectiveness of the people responsible for enacting the leader's vision to produce the desired results. It is the people who make the difference in success or failure, and in so doing, they are the most important aspect of a leader's responsibility to her organization. Without great people there is no great company.

I appreciate Terry McDougall providing me with the thought-provoking subject matter for this lesson learned. I hope I did justice in relating the story and in covering the overall meaning with some semblance of empathy. I admire Terry for all she is as a happy mom, wife, successful executive coach, and best-selling author.

But I admire Terry the most for how her leadership actions as related in this experience reflect on her as a person.

Terry is a great human being.

> **Compassion:** Sympathetic consciousness of others' distress together with a desire to alleviate it. The meaning of compassion is recognizing the suffering of others and then taking action to help.

> **Leadership in Action:** You will experience the need for compassion throughout your leadership endeavors. These moments will present themselves periodically and at times under familiar circumstances. True leaders know when to act and also what appropriate action to take. They have a

clear and focused vision in this regard.

Be aware, and keep your eyes open.

LESSON #4: SHOW UP

Eighty percent of success is just showing up.
—Woody Allen

Ninety percent of life is just showing up.
—President George H. W. Bush

Winters in Chicago can be brutal. The snow, wind, and be-low-zero temperatures lead to icy roads, frozen car batteries, and significantly less than ideal travel conditions. In severe blizzard conditions, long layovers, delays, and cancelations are common at the airports. I've experienced these difficult travel conditions on numerous occasions trying to get to important business meetings across the country.

Many times I fought through the inclination to turn my car around, tell the limo driver to take me back home, cancel the meeting, change the appointment, or as we used to say in college, "bag it." Only once do I remember actually changing my travel date because of weather, and that was due to a hurricane going into southern Florida. No one was flying into the sunshine state at that time. I canceled my plans due to illness a few scant times, but for the majority of my career, I stuck it out, hung in there, persevered, and paid the price of business travel.

Delays, layovers, and cancelations due to inclement weather are all part of the grind of business travel and can lead to overcrowded terminals at the airport. And worst of all, the over crowdedness can lead to sold-out concessions. How can one be stuck in a Chicago airport and not have an option for a slice of pizza? That, my friends, is totally un-American. Yet it happens. Have you ever been inconvenienced in an airport due to a delay only to find the concessions closed or serving a limited menu? Yes, you can relate. You've been there, done that, certainly don't look forward to having to do it again.

Fortunately, my days of being a road warrior are long since passed, but the memories of slogging through one airport after another on a weekly basis during my sales trainer and sales management days are well ingrained. It was grueling at times, yet I wouldn't trade those memories for anything. The experience of being an "at the ready" business traveler certainly prepared me for dealing with anything the most overcrowded spring-break-vacationer-packed airport could throw at me. Screaming kids and college students eager to visit warmer climates were no match for me and my headphones. Block them out, take in the sights, enjoy my tunes. Or I would go the old-fashioned route and read. Nothing like burying myself in a book to pass the time and continue my lifelong learner quest. Third option was to pull out the laptop and work. Depending on my priorities, the third option became my first choice quite often. Get the work done, then relax.

That's the way I've always been—task-oriented, work first, a *get things done* kind of guy. This characteristic proved beneficial numerous times in my managerial days. It provided me with a purpose. I had to get the job done. I had to finish what I had started. I had to correct the things I saw that needed correcting. I had to make my list and cross off the tasks as they were accomplished. I had to train others to do their jobs, and I had to teach them the right way, the best way, and the fastest way. I had to respond to those emails promptly. (I would later learn that being the first person to respond with an answer doesn't always equate with being the person who responds first with the right answer.) I had to develop my obsessive-compulsive disorder. Yes, had to, no pun intended. OCD was the result of years of business-related repetitive thoughts about being committed to getting the work done. Maybe it developed because of fear of failure or maybe because of a burning desire to succeed. Most likely it developed as a combination of both. But the greatest influence on my OCD from my perspective was my thought of responsibility to my organization, coworkers, and customers. I could not accept being the person who was vilified for letting them down. I could not accept that as an outcome of my actions. I had to be there for them. I had to. I had to go to work. I had to. There is a big difference between "I had to" and "I want to." It took me years to understand how to make this work for my mental health. Thankfully, I worked for organizations that provided me with the opportunities that helped me "want to" do my job.

There are times, however, that still haunt me, times I put work ahead of family. I had to go to work. I had an obligation. I had a commitment. I had a position of authority and leadership that required me to prioritize my actions in the name of business and career success. I had not yet learned the value of commitment in the proper sense of family first, business second, balance of the life-career journey as a requirement of happiness and personal success. I made several poor choices along those lines early in my business career and worked hard to avoid those same mistakes when similar circumstances occurred.

A person who reminded me of my exuberance for work yet one who also manages to have a satisfying work-life balance is Kelly Crabb. I've known Kelly Crabb since she was Kelly Ellison as we had the pleasure of working together at DeVry University back in the early 2000s. Kelly is currently the vice president of global sales at an educational assessment solutions provider that serves institutions of learning around the world and is based in Denver, Colorado. It does not surprise me at all that Kelly is an extraordinarily successful businessperson with a huge level of responsibility to her organization. From the early stages of her career, I identified Kelly as a go-getter. Her work ethic was incredible. Her commitment and dedication to getting the job done were second to none. If you were to look in the dictionary, Kelly's picture could be there under several entries: "commitment," "dedication," "work ethic," "determination." Her level of commitment was in the same range as mine, and as she was a young person focused on getting the job done, this level of intensity led to an unacceptable level of stress for Kelly at times. It took its toll, but it also provided Kelly with experience on how to appropriately handle commitment and still balance her life at the same time.

When asked about her thoughts on leadership for the purpose of contributing to this book, Kelly related the story of her experience as a newly appointed business development director. Her consultative sales and leadership experience led to her being the right fit for this assignment, and Kelly pursued it with the anticipated vim and vigor, as her supervisors expected. Within a few months, Kelly positioned her organization as a finalist for a multiyear, high revenue contract and was asked to present the final proposal for services in person to the prospective client's senior leadership in Grand Forks, North Dakota. As this was Kelly's first major presentation in her new role, her vice president of sales, Gene, would accompany her to the presentation. In order to do so, Gene would fly from his home base in Charlottesville, Virginia, to Grand Forks the evening prior to the presentation. They would use the evening to prep for the presentation, which was scheduled for 9:00 a.m. the next morning.

Kelly flew from Denver and arrived in Grand Forks without issue and while reviewing her presentation for the next day, received this message from Gene; "Flight is delayed due to thunderstorms. Not looking good." This was Gene's first opportunity to observe Kelly in a high-reward presentation mode, so while getting prepared, she hoped Gene's flight situation would work out. Not only did she want to have Gene observe her presentation, but she also wanted Gene there for support and to utilize his experience as a key selling point with the prospective client. *It will work out*, she thought to herself.

Time passed. No word from Gene. *Perhaps all was well, and he is on his way*, Kelly thought. But then the text message from Gene appeared: "Flight canceled." Kelly's heart pounded. Thoughts of her having to go it alone raced through her mind. *What questions will they ask? What if they press me for a decision beyond my scope of authority? How would Gene address them? Stay calm, breathe; I will handle it*, she thought.

Moments passed, and another text arrived from Gene: "Flying to Chicago, and then to Minneapolis; will drive to Grand Forks." It was exhausting for Kelly just thinking about two flights and a five-hour car ride the night before a major presentation scheduled for nine the next morning. Kelly was incredibly grateful that Gene was attempting this trip.

While excited about the possibility that Gene would *show up*, Kelly did not want to get her hopes up as she knew the travel schedule would have to go off without a hitch. Gene was boarding a flight at 10:00 p.m. from Chicago to Minneapolis, which meant that he would be navigating the five-hour drive to Grand Forks after midnight with arrival approximately between 5:00 a.m. and 6:00 a.m. Barely room to spare to be ready for a 9:00 a.m. presentation!

As Gene was going on nearly twenty-four hours without sleep, he decided to stop at a hotel about an hour outside of Grand Forks to get some rest. Kelly did not know this until it was 8:00 a.m. presentation morning and she had not heard from Gene. She called him, no answer. On the second attempt, Gene answered and muttered, "Hello." Kelly, doing her best to suppress the concern in her voice, asked, "Gene, are you in Grand Forks? We have an hour to presentation time!" The adrenaline prompted from the urgency in Kelly's voice jolted Gene into action.

He would do what he had to, get suited up, and *show up*.

Notorious for being early and overprepared for meetings, Kelly arrived early to the presentation, had everything set up accordingly, and began introducing herself to a room full of key stakeholders. They were already there, early, ready to go, waiting to get started. No Gene. Being late to this presentation would not be an acceptable situation. This client held their punctuality in high esteem. While the client was trying to show understanding for Gene's travel dilemma, being late wasn't the best way to make a first impression. No Gene. Kelly did not want to start the presentation without Gene, and it certainly would look awkward if he entered the meeting room after she started. The only option available? Stall. If there ever was a time for a song and dance before the dog and pony, this was it. What could Kelly do?

She bargained for time, and an additional five minutes was granted. Five minutes was not enough. Thinking fast, Kelly recalled that a parking pass was required for certain areas of the parking lot. She requested one from the meeting coordinator and made the trek from the meeting room to her car in the parking lot, where much to her astonishment and joy, there was Gene pulling up in his rental car.

Gene showed up!

Kelly's level of respect for this road warrior multiplied twofold in the five minutes it took her to get him from his car to the meeting room coffee bar. Following a large sip of coffee, Gene was at the podium, opening the meeting with introductions and a resounding kickoff in as professional a manner as Kelly had ever witnessed.

Gene showed up, and delivered.

One can only appreciate Gene's dedication if one has experienced similar circumstances. The commitment to showing up resonates with those of us who can relate. There was never a doubt in Gene's mind that he would make every effort to get to the meeting. He wasn't going to let poor travel conditions prevent him from supporting his new business development person. But Gene also knew that his actions would go a lot further than just the physical support he could provide at the presentation. He knew his dedicated actions and commitment to Kelly would make a lasting impression that she would reflect upon and carry forward in her commitment to her clients, to her team, and to her career.

Kelly took that valuable lesson to heart.

In her own words: "Gene's tremendous effort to *show up* and support the first high-stakes sales presentation that we delivered together, despite the incredible challenges he faced, demonstrated exemplary leadership in business and also served as a model for how I want to *show up* for those who depend on me personally."

As I mentioned earlier, it doesn't surprise me that Kelly is an extraordinarily successful businessperson. But it also doesn't surprise me that Kelly is also a loving mom with a huge level of personal responsibility and commitment to her husband and children. While she travels for business on a regular basis, she's discovered she can balance her dedication and commitment to her family with her business career.

I know this, as evidenced by a story Kelly shared of her own challenging travel situation and her response to this challenge. While in Boston for a conference, Kelly received a text that her flight home to Denver that day was canceled. No big deal— she would just wait it out and get on another flight when it was available. Except there was one problem with that line of thinking. She realized that her then seven-year-old daughter Ella was in a theater performance the next day, and Kelly had promised her she would be back from her business trip in time to attend the performance.

Kelly remembered the lesson learned example of Gene and took immediate action. She drove to the Boston airport and managed to get the last seat on a flight to Baltimore. From Baltimore she would have a last option to catch a flight to Denver with a brief stop in Dallas. Boston to Baltimore to Dallas to Denver. Certainly not the direct route or the easiest of travel schedule, but this was the only way to get home, to *show up*. And Kelly had to get home, had to show up. Kelly's commitment to career and family are both extraordinarily strong. In this situation her little girl needed her mom to be there. After all, she made the commitment, she made the promise, she was going to make the effort to get there.

The late arrival in Denver put Kelly home in the wee hours of the morning. She was totally exhausted but relieved she had made it home, and all thoughts of "bagging it" were left far behind when Ella burst into Kelly's bedroom early after sunrise, excited to see her mom, threw her arms around her, and squealed "You made it for my play!" It doesn't get any more rewarding. Kelly recognized Ella's reaction and most notably, that her daughter felt important.

As a leader asks for the respect of his or her team, a parent asks for much the same of his or her children. Yet that respect is earned by actions, not by words. The concept of *showing up* for employees, teams, coworkers, family, and simply everyone that relies on you is primary. It is the foundation of effective responsibility and leadership.

Showing up ranks high on the list of numerous obligations as a leader. The expectations of others are high when it comes to knowing their leader is reliable, regardless of the situation or circumstances. A leader will be presented with numerous and various opportunities to mentor, teach, coach, observe, partake, and set the example as a role model for those who have high expectations of reliability. A true leader knows that *showing up* to interact with the team is a necessary and impactful requirement and accepts that responsibility without question. Much like a true loving parent knows there is nothing more important in the eyes of a child than having that parent be there for them, the parent willingly takes on the responsibility and follows through with supporting actions.

Thank you, Kelly, for sharing your story and for prompting this lesson learned.

Showing up is an important lesson learned in leadership and complements the other lessons in this book. It is one I had to write about with appreciation. I had to write about it with respect. I had to write with complete understanding of the importance of leadership support and parental commitment. I had to write this lesson learned.

I just had to.

Presence: The fact or condition of being present; the bearing, carriage, or air of a person, especially a stately or distinguished bearing, a noteworthy quality of poise and effectiveness

Leadership in Action: True leaders know the value of professional presence and are always aware of the impression they leave on their coworkers. This is especially true when the leader walks in late to a meeting.

The silence can be deafening.

LESSON #5: GET AHEAD OF THE CURVE

*It is easy to sit up and take notice. What is
difficult is getting up and taking action.*
—Honoré de Balzac

The *Merriam-Webster* dictionary defines "complacency" as "self-satisfaction especially when accompanied by unawareness of actual dangers or deficiencies. When it comes to safety, complacency can be dangerous."

What *Merriam-Webster* does not mention is that when it comes to business leadership, complacency can not only be dangerous, but it can also be career-ending for the leader and spell the end of the business as well. Being unusually unaware or uniformed is not an excuse for failure to achieve desired results, nor is it accepted as a reason for poor performance. Being unaware or uniformed is not to be used as a crutch. "I didn't know," "No one told me," "I wasn't aware of the circumstances" just don't fly when it comes to leadership accountability.

In simple terms, ignorance is not a legitimate excuse.

The only thing worse than being unaware or uniformed as an organizational leader is being aware and informed and failing to act on the information.

Being aware and informed is a prerequisite to being a great leader. The leader must take an active approach to investigation, to finding out what is going on, to engaging in and understanding the pulse of the business. This applies internally within the organization, externally with customers, market influences, and conditions, and also includes key shareholders and stakeholders. Leaders have an unquenchable thirst for information that allows them to understand their business, their customer's business, their competition's business, and the influencing factors in all of those scenarios. They live to be informed to understand. And ultimately, while being aware and informed provides the leader with the opportunity to know, learn, and understand people, situations, and influences, it is the leader's ability to know what to do with the information and how to act on the information that makes the difference between success or failure.

Again, in simple terms, information granted is only as good as the leader who uses it wisely. Information not acted upon is information wasted.

Yet if we look at a few examples in recent history, it is evident the leaders of certain organizations settled into a self-satisfactory level of complacency in their roles and thereby perpetrated complacency throughout the organization, thus leading to its demise. Organizations like Blockbuster, Toys "R" Us, and Polaroid failed from an innovation standpoint, but more importantly they failed by not recognizing new technology and for not using their well-established organizations as leverage to take full advantage of new technology and thereby adapt to change for continued growth. Had Blockbuster not been complacent with their big-box video rental business, they would have directed their efforts to digital technology and ultimately could have become what Netflix is today. Toys "R" Us missed out on the opportunity to create an online shopping market and potentially could have been the preferred toy provider, a role taken up by online service provider Amazon. And Polaroid, stuck in their instant black-and-white photo processing business, failed to recognize the potential of digital printing, and lost out on becoming today's Instagram.

The leaders of these companies failed to see the signals of a changing marketplace and ultimately failed to act on those signals. These are examples of companies that dominated their respective markets, generated amazing revenue and profit, maintained an untouchable reputation and brand, and basically operated a legitimate top-of-the-mind awareness monopoly. Fat cats with little need to pursue innovation. Their mousetrap was the marketplace mousetrap. Nothing could change their state of affairs; nothing could impact their business. Or so they thought.

One such company that could be the cover photo for a book on organizational complacency was photographic roll-film maker Eastman Kodak. At one time Kodak was the world's largest producer of camera roll film and dominated the US market. Almost everyone using a 35 mm camera to take vacation, family, business, commercial, and professional photography used Kodak film to take those photos. While Kodak faced some competition from Japanese company Fuji, their dominance in the United States was evident. Kodak was synonymous with taking photos; hence the phrase "Kodak Moment" was coined.

As the competition from Fuji increased in the 1980s, there loomed an even more pressing threat to Kodak in the form of technology. More specifically, digital technology. Kodak scientists and research people accurately forecasted that the use of digital technology was rapidly becoming a threat to the roll-film business. Literally, film was going to be replaced; it would become obsolete. There was going to be a better mousetrap, and it was going to happen soon. The marketplace would inevitably embrace this new, innovative, and easy-to-use technology, and Kodak would need to change their business focus. So what happened? In Kodak's case, nothing.

Kodak researchers were actually the ones who developed the digital technology to replace film. In fact, the first digital camera was invented by a Kodak engineer way back in 1975. Filmless photography was going to be the next biggest thing. Filmless photography would disrupt the status quo, revolutionize the photography industry, and impact the marketplace in ways unimaginable at that time.

What did Kodak leadership do when they learned of this potential blockbuster technology? They did nothing imaginative for the betterment of the business. Unless you consider ignoring the information to be doing something. They not only ignored the information, but they also kept quiet about it, as evidenced by their lack of willingness to explore, develop, and improve digital technology throughout the late 1990s and early 2000s. That is really hard to believe, but it is true, as evidenced by Kodak's bankruptcy several years later.

Their leadership was so emboldened by the current state and success of their roll-film business at the time digital technology was introduced they became complacent and ignorant about any form of threat to that business.

Even a threat that could be viewed as an immense opportunity, a threat invented in their own organization!

They failed to listen to their own employees, failed to understand the impact digital technology would have on their current business, and more importantly, failed to understand the impact on their future business. They didn't own their leadership responsibility to be strategic and innovative, have a long-term vision, and grow an organization. They settled with status quo complacency. They stuck to their traditionalist methods. They didn't act on the innovative information provided to them by their own employees. They went bankrupt.

They had the opportunity but failed to get ahead of the curve.

Kodak suffered from a failure to implement a culture of innovative thinking, or at least of acceptance of innovative thinking, one that was open to change and flexible enough to adapt to technological advances and marketplace demands and act on those influences. If the leadership of an organization drives the organization's culture, Kodak leadership failed to establish a culture of appreciation for innovation; had it been instilled, it would have saved the company. It was the leaders, not the employees, who failed to innovate.

When I read the Kodak business failure history, I found it hard to fathom that the leaders of the Kodak organization could have been so blind to the opportunity and simply placed their organization at risk via their own stubborn mentality of thinking that film would always be the number one choice of consumers. Obviously, they were afraid the new technology would cannibalize their current business. This is a perfect example of shortsighted thinking, ignorance to innovation, and ultimately, leadership complacency.

True leaders do not have time to be complacent. They are too busy engaging in their organization's business at every possible level internally and externally to get a handle on what's going on in order to prepare for potential threats but also to look for new opportunities. While it seems a daunting task to be cognizant of so many potential influences and informational sources, the savvy leader knows the best way to stay informed is to have a network of highly trusted advisers to assist in the information gathering and ultimately in the action decision-making.

True leaders look for ways to get ahead of the curve.

One such leader who made the effort to get ahead of the curve is my friend and former business associate Chris Krull. Chris and I have had a long friendship, having worked together in the late 1990s. I came to appreciate Chris for his keen business sense and work ethic, but really enjoyed his personality and quick wit. A cancer survivor, Chris is one of those types of people who would not let as serious a situation as having been diagnosed with cancer impact his positive attitude and outlook on life. I'm sure he had numerous difficult, challenging days during his cancer treatment, but never did I witness or hear of him having a bad attitude about his situation. Chris is strong in this regard.

It also helped our friendship that Chris is a huge baseball and hockey fan, much like me, although his allegiance to baseball's St. Louis Cardinals and hockey's St. Louis Blues is in direct conflict to my cheering for the Chicago Cubs and the Chicago Blackhawks. Two of the greatest rivalries in all of sports are the ones involving the Cardinals-Cubs and Blues-Blackhawks. The baseball rivalry has existed since the late 1800s, and the hockey rivalry, younger yet just as intense, since the late 1960s. It doesn't get much better than these rivalries, and both Chris and I have our own stories and experiences in this regard. While we cheer for direct competitors, our overall love of baseball and hockey have outweighed our competitive loyalty and helped us bond as friends.

As a regional director of sales at a nationwide direct mail company, Chris was charged with ensuring the profitability of the Saint Louis metropolitan market, one of the company's flagship operations. He was also charged with protecting the business relationship with the three base players in the St. Louis market, who contributed 40 percent of the market's overall revenue. The viability of Chris's organization's direct mail program in the St. Louis market came from three independent grocery store chains. Without any one of these customers, Chris's business would suffer a major revenue hit. If one of these customers left for another advertising option, the others would most likely follow suit to keep up with the competition.

To his advantage, Chris enjoyed a long history of a well-established business relationship with each of the three base players. They were excellent customers and were treated as such by Chris and his team of professional marketing, sales, and customer service representatives. Business was good. In fact, it was so good that the direct mail business and entity that Chris represented was close to being the only game in town. The competition was not a threat since they couldn't get their collective advertising act together and certainly couldn't penetrate the relationship Chris maintained with the three base players.

This situation presented the perfect opportunity for complacency. What could possibly disrupt the longstanding relationship and profitability? The customers were happy, and Chris's company was happy with the results.

In fact, Chris's company was so satisfied with the results and their hold on the marketplace that they leveraged their dominance by consistently limiting the three base players to one-year advertising contracts. One-year contracts that included a price increase each time the contract was renewed. Basically Chris's company set the price and allowed the three base customers the "privilege" of advertising with the company. After all, they really didn't have any other legitimate option for advertising their grocery stores with the level of market coverage and household penetration that the direct mail company could deliver. So while there were annual negotiations regarding the price increases in the new contracts, Chris held the leverage.

Except, Chris didn't view his business only along those lines. While the profitability was great, taking advantage of a relationship-first customer is short-term thinking. All it would take to destroy the monopoly Chris' company enjoyed at the time was for a new competitor to enter the market with equal or superior advertising distribution, household penetration, and more advantageous advertising pricing, and the big three customers could easily become the big three former customers.

The threat was on the horizon, and Chris recognized this scenario as one that if it came to fruition, would severely damage his company but also could cost him his job.

Now think of this example as it relates to the higher-ups at Kodak who in all their corporate glory were basking in the by-product of their market dominance. They enjoyed the status quo because it worked for them and their profit goals. They were complacent in their thinking that nothing could go wrong.

Chris was faced with similar circumstances—leadership higher up in the organization who liked the fact that they could leverage one-year agreements to their advantage and basically set the price for market advertising without fear of losing business to a competitor. They never could accept the fact that a new entity with superior management skills, professional salespeople hungry for growth, and a support and logistics team second to none would ever challenge their dominance in the St. Louis market. It just couldn't happen. Who would be so bold as to challenge the status quo? Who could possibly disrupt their current business model? Their direction to Chris was simple—leave things as is and keep raking in the profit.

Except Chris wouldn't leave it alone. He was in tune with the marketplace. He was aware of the competition and their efforts to ramp up their game. He knew they were planning a bold initiative to strategically attack Chris's three base customers with significantly discounted pricing offers backed up by legitimate household market coverage. Chris knew the competition was coming for his business. He knew he had to get ahead of the curve.

His challenge was to convince the higher-ups in the organization to agree to allow him to sign the three base customers to long-term contracts. Contracts that protected both the customer's interests by limiting price increases and Chris's business interests in maintaining the all-important 40 percent revenue stream. It would seem to the casual observer that these long-term contracts would be an obvious strategy to enforce a customer-centric and collaborative sales relationship approach. Totally makes sense, right?

Not to the higher up leadership and the finance people in Chris's organization. They were of the opinion that the competition would not be able to get their act together in a relatively short period of time and took the position of "Let's wait until the threat gets closer." That's about as good a strategy as it would be to tell the captain of the *Titanic* to wait until the iceberg gets closer! Yes, we know it's out there, but we want to be absolutely certain it actually is in position to hit us and tear the hull of our ship from bow to stern before we change course. Good grief.

We would rather be complacent in our thinking than accept, adapt, and change.

Fortunately, Chris is as tenacious a businessperson as he is a skilled negotiator. The two characteristics go hand in hand, and when Chris had an opportunity to present his case to the key influencers and decision makers in the company, he was able to build a business case complete with supportive documentation and facts that significantly impacted his audience's decision-making. They not only recognized and understood the threat to the St. Louis market profitability, but they also did something unheard of at the time. They directed Chris to act on his instinct, market knowledge, and business sense to lock up the three base customers with long-term contracts that were reasonable for both entities.

Complacency eliminated.

With renewed enthusiasm and a commitment to prove his hypothesis to be the correct business strategy, Chris worked diligently with his sales team to change a mindset and ultimately improve already acceptable performance. He wanted his team to go from good to great, and this was a perfect opportunity to initiate an innovative approach to challenging the status quo. With this engaged effort, Chris and his team were able to secure multiyear commitments from the three base customers in a relatively short period of time, thereby establishing a much-appreciated new-found relationship between customer and seller. And in so doing, Chris blocked the competition from delivering on their plans to jeopardize his well-established business, and his job.

Chris won out by recognizing a serious business threat, understanding the ramifications from several different perspectives, and presenting a strategic business case that changed the thinking of a complacent organization.

Some of you may be thinking that the higher-ups and the finance people knew all along they would get to long-term contracts sooner or later and just wanted to let Chris think it was his idea to implement the strategy. Not so. Having worked in the same organization as Chris for several years, I can personally vouch for the absolute micromanagement control and complacent thinking that prevailed in the organization. Living in fear of yearly increased postal rates to carry direct mail packages provoked that micromanagement approach. A long-term contract could in actuality force the company to deliver the direct mail pieces at a loss if postage rates exceeded the contract's provisions. What Chris accomplished was monumental, disruptive, and innovative.

But above all it was a perfect example of a leader taking the initiative and acting on information. It was the perfect example of leadership in action. It was the perfect example of getting ahead of the curve and not allowing complacency to sidetrack or distract from a leader's commitment and dedication to continuous improvement.

Others may have maintained the status quo and enjoyed the fruits of current labor without having a thought to the future. Others may have relished the knowledge that their current situation was satisfactorily acceptable. Others may have relaxed and waited for the iceberg to get closer. Others may have taken the Kodak approach and ignored the information.

But Chris Krull is not like others. He is a leader who used this opportunity to act accordingly for what proved to be not only his benefit, but that of his team and his organization.

Not bad for a St. Louis Cardinals fan. Definitely above expectations for a St. Louis Blues fan. Or as Chris put it, "This is exactly what should be expected from a St. Louis Cardinals and St. Louis Blues fan."

Our competitive rivalry won't get in the way of our friendship—or the significance of this lesson learned.

Way to get ahead of the curve, Chris Krull.

Resiliency: An ability to recover from or adjust easily to adversity or change.

Leadership in Action: All leaders experience a unique level of adversity throughout the course of their undertakings, yet it is the genuinely great ones who are resilient in their efforts to adapt, change, pivot, and move on toward the completion of their overarching goal.

Demonstrating resiliency is easy, and kind of like quitting chocolate.

I've done it hundreds of times.

LESSON #6: LEADERSHIP AND TRUST

The best executive is the one who has sense enough to pick good people to do what he wants done and self-restraint enough to keep from meddling with them while they do it.
—Theodore Roosevelt

Sales training facilitators throughout the world have long proposed the answers to two basic questions as starting points to help fledgling salespeople learn the basics of selling. First question: Why do people buy? Second question: Who do they buy from? (From whom do they buy? if you want to be formal.)

The answers to those questions are formulated in several basic statements:

They need to solve a problem or meet a need.

They see the product or service as beneficial to their interests.

They see the product or service as functional or practical (not necessarily logical) to their intended use.

They feel the prestige and/or emotion associated with buying the product or service.

And perhaps equally important, they realize a solution or benefit to themselves and/or to their organization.

Also in general, people buy a product or service from salespeople whom they know, like, trust, view as helpful, or see as embodying any and all of those qualities.

Most importantly, people buy from those who understand the customer's personal or business situation and who act in the customer's best interests.

Tradition and simplicity abound in answering the two questions listed in the opening paragraph. However, you and I know the selling-buying process is much more complicated. The customer is more complex, the salesperson is much more knowledgeable, the options of what to buy and the competition among sellers are in many cases unlimited.

> *Yet, to summarize and bring the process down to its most grounded level, people buy for their reasons and their reasons alone. They will buy from others when they recognize the benefit to themselves or their organization and are convinced the value associated with the purchase is worth the price.*

They make the decision based on their beliefs and no one else's. Somewhere along the way, they determine that the person who is guiding them through the buying process can be trusted throughout this whole situation. Unless they are buying something online, in which case they only have themselves to trust for their own decisions.

Trust. Simple in meaning yet complex in reality in business and personal relationships. Much like in ethics, there is no gray area when it comes to trust. Either you believe in a person and place confidence in their intent, or you don't. The decision to trust someone is entirely up to you, based on your assessment of interactions with the person and your observation of their actions toward others. Trust can be established by preceding reputation or by reference, yet is really only gained by personal experience and practical observation.

Coworkers and business associates gain trust in leadership based on observed and participatory interactions between the leader and the constituents. Leaders earn trust in the same regard. This two-way premise is sound for both internal and external scenarios. So while it is imperative for a salesperson to gain a customer's trust throughout the buying process, so too is it imperative that the leader gain an organization's (people's) trust in order to fully implement and execute desired strategies. Without an organization's trust and support for a strategic platform, that platform is doomed to fail.

So, the big question: Assuming trust from others is a critical factor in implementing strategy, executing that strategy, and delivering results, how does a leader gain trust?

To answer that question, I went to an expert in sales, not an expert in leadership. I did this intentionally to get the perspective of the coworker, the associate, the constituent who interacts with the leader and observes the leader's actions, the person who will determine if the leader is to be trusted. I was absolutely thrilled when Rob Jolles agreed to spend some time with me and help me address this question. A little bit of Rob's background first.

Rob Jolles is a world-renowned best-selling author, professional speaker, sales trainer, sales professional, and consultant. His consulting services in the areas of sales training, business coaching, executive mentoring, and influencing others are highly sought-after. Known for his wit and wisdom, Rob is a big proponent of customer-centered selling. In fact one of his best-selling books is named just that.

Customer Centered Selling: Eight Steps to Success From the World's Best Sales Force, published in 2000 and updated to a second edition in 2009, is founded in Rob's experience as a successful salesperson during his selling days with Xerox corporation. This book includes material and case studies consistent with Rob's focus on anticipating and influencing behavior. His sales methodology teaches a systemic, repeatable approach that allows the salesperson to understand the buying process through the customer's viewpoint.

For the purposes of answering the question at hand, I was most interested in Rob's 2018 publication *Why People Don't Believe You: Building Credibility From the Inside Out*. The book's title is the premise of trust itself and a directive that all salespeople should take to heart, one that any leader should embrace.

While Rob and I spent a great deal of time during our Zoom interview talking about the principles of sales, sales training, and best practices in the true art of selling, we eventually got around to the matter at hand. I asked Rob to tell me about his sales managers at New York Life when he first started out as a twenty-two-year-old life insurance salesperson, and then at Xerox, where he mastered a selling process, became extraordinarily successful, and then ultimately realized and acted upon his calling as an entrepreneur to teach others how to influence and build relationships.

Rob answered my question with a true sales professional's response. How does a leader gain trust? Rob's answer: "Are their actions supporting my goals, and do they have my interest at heart?" In other words, a leader—or in Rob's case, a sales manager—gains trust via actions that are in direct support of the coworker—in Rob's case, a salesperson—and his goals of building a relationship with a potential customer in order to satisfy the needs of that customer.

Brilliant. It is without doubt a similar, if not the exact, question that goes through the mind of a prospective customer when in the throngs of a salesperson's presentation. "Do they have my best interests and the best interests of my company in mind as they are trying to sell me their product or service?"

The leader earns credibility, gains trust by supporting the coworker to successfully do their job. The prospective customer gains trust in the salesperson whose actions support the customer's best interests.

Absolutely brilliant, and simple.

> *A leader gains trust via actions that are in direct support of the coworker's intent. A salesperson gains a prospective customer's trust based on actions in direct support of the customer's best interests.*

Of course, critical to this premise being acted upon is the legitimacy of the coworker's intent. Obviously, a leader will not support intent that is not appropriate or in line with the core values of the organization. In much the same way, a customer will not trust a salesperson whose actions are self-serving and in direct conflict with the prospective customer's intent.

To add emphasis to this premise, let us examine some of the key qualities and concepts by which leaders build trust:

- **Credible**—being credible is founded in being reliable to the extent that as a leader you will do what you say you are going to do and will do so when you say you are going to do it. You can be trusted to be reliable.

- **Transparent**—there will be times when a leader must withhold information in order to protect people's privacy, yet for the most part being transparent about company policy, standing, direction, or endorsement should be an open and visible undertaking.

- **Partners**—true leaders recognize the power of collaboration and are in tune with their coworkers. "We're in this together" is cliché yet commands a leader's attention when faced with employees who expect the same level of unity that the leader expects from coworkers. Employees do not want to be sold on the leader's agenda. They want a say and want to be included in the process. They want *in* to be able to *buy in*.

- **Respectful**—leaders are cognizant of others in all regards and situations and do not let their title get in the way of their intentions to treat others as they would be treated. They are benevolent and have others' best interests in mind in their interactions.

- **Truth**—telling the truth goes hand in hand with building trust, and being honest in telling the facts provides evidence for others to observe and by which to determine trust.

- **Relationships**—it's difficult to earn trust and respect without having a mutually beneficial relationship. Spending time with coworkers outside of the workplace provides an opportunity to get to know them as people and helps the leader understand their individual situation. Getting a coworker to open up about their personal situation may be another matter, but it is something a leader should attempt.

- **Encourage**—others are more likely to trust and engage with a leader who coaches with positive support rather than one who commands in a derogatory manner

- **Accountable**—the leader who takes responsibility for strategy, direction, actions, and results allows others to view them as being committed to owning their work.

- **Reward**—the leader is always willing to recognize and reward others for their contributions to the benefit of fellow employees and the benefit of the organization. Acting with sincerity in this manner provides legitimacy and opens the door for a trusting environment.

- **Competent**—a leader gains trust by being aware of their own skill set and goes about doing their job in a well-respected and efficient manner. The leader is good at what she does. The leader is productive and does the job as expected by the coworkers. Leaders gain trust by acting and demonstrating the characteristics as listed above, but they also gain trust via their inactions in certain areas including:

  - **Avoiding the rumor mill**—leaders gain trust by living in reality and have no time to engage in organizational gossip or innuendo. They work in fact-based reality and set the example for their coworkers by staying on the straight and narrow.

  - **Avoiding badmouthing**—leaders gain trust by speaking highly of people in the organization who deserve acknowledgment and recognition and will not speak down to others.

  - **Avoiding playing favorites**—all are treated equally

yet as unique individuals. No one is better or more in favor with the leader. The leader is careful in actions to ensure that perception is reality.

While the abovementioned bullet points provide definition to a leader's means of gaining and building trust, there is one additional critical area of skill a person must be cognizant of and implement appropriately in order to be viewed as a leader and influencer.

The leader must return trust in a like manner in order to be trusted.

Therefore the leader must be willing to empower and allow those in his stead to perform their given assignments without engaging in overbearing inspections and critique. To fully gain their trust, the leader in turn trusts his coworkers to do their jobs and takes on the role of servant, supportive adviser when needed. No one really likes to be micromanaged, regardless of organizational level. The collaborative leader allows for innovation, productivity, and camaraderie to occur by trusting others, just as trust is asked of them. Much is to be said for the leader who recognizes an exemplary skill set in coworkers and allows them the freedom to perform their function accordingly. Leaders who work in this manner build trust as a long-lasting two-way proposition.

To further build on the sales leader–salesperson trust factor as a long-term two-way relationship, I asked another person

I highly respect for her opinion on this matter. This person is family and a little bit closer to home as she is my niece-in-law Melissa Buttacavoli Kulawiak (a name providing a fairly strong test of the English alphabet and pronunciation).

Melissa is currently the vice president of business development at Epsilon, a high-profile marketing organization in Chicago. Prior to Epsilon, Melissa spent nearly twenty years with a major direct mail company, getting promoted several times along the way while working her way up to a vice president of retail sales title. Melissa is street-smart, intelligent, and respected for having worked diligently to get to where she is today. She earned the respect of her associates by doing her job in a proficient manner and used those actions to build trust within her organization.

Her comments regarding leadership trust complement the two-way street philosophy. The commitment a sales leader makes to the personal development and success of the salesperson is returned enthusiastically when the salesperson realizes the leader is working with the best interests of the salesperson in mind. The support is not only appreciated, but it also becomes a foundation for the relationship. It is easy to build trust in this regard. Both leader and salesperson are helping each other to be successful and thereby have each other's success in mind.

In her own words, "Salespeople are motivated by many things, but in the end it comes down to a scale of success. They want to be part of something bigger and still reap the individual rewards. Knowing they have a leader that is committed to helping them grow and develop is often enough to motivate them to want to give it everything they've got and go the extra mile when needed."

Melissa's comments summarize my thought process about leadership and trust. Would you give it all you've got and go the extra mile for someone you didn't trust? Would you do as much for someone who didn't have your best interests, your goal achievement, and your success in mind? Would you demonstrate the same level or even a greater level of commitment to your job, your organization, or yourself if you worked with a leader who didn't reciprocate the same level of dedication?

In essence, a leader who commits to supporting coworkers, peers, and associates in their best interests, positive intents, and individual development is on the right path to gaining trust. A leader begins to build trust by being competent, credible, and benevolent. But a leader must also know that in order to be truly effective, there must be a commitment to others. Commitment to others provides peace of mind for both leader and associates. It is not the end all be all, secret sauce for a leader to earn trust, yet commitment to others is a darned good starting point.

> **Trust:** Assured reliance on the character, ability, strength, or truth of someone or something; one in which confidence is placed

> **Leadership in Action:** There is no better example of leadership in action than trusting your di-

rect reports to arrange for client entertainment. You know they will stay within company rules and abide by the client's company rules as well. What may challenge your trust in them, however, is your reaction to approving their expense accounts.

"You spent what?" is not recommended.

LESSON #7: THE LADDER GOES BOTH WAYS

If you want to see the true measure of a man, watch how he treats his inferiors, not his equals.
—J. K. Rowling

You can tell a lot about a person simply by observing how they treat the restaurant waitstaff. Now, I'm not sure who said this specifically about a waitstaff, or where I heard it first, but I agree wholeheartedly. Being ugly to a waitstaff tells a lot about that person's personality and their value system. A person who feels or believes themselves to be superior to a waitstaff and demonstrates their belief either verbally, physically, or both perceives the waitperson to be in a subordinate role. This aristocratically inclined person adheres to a situational value system. This person changes his characterological approach based on the perceived status of the person he is dealing with in a given situation.

I have observed people of this nature being absolutely flat-out ugly to the waitperson for the smallest of missteps, like forgetting to fill the water glasses or putting too much or not enough ice in the water glasses. Maybe the person was just having a bad day and the slightest irritation set them off in a tirade, but regardless of the personal situation, berating the waitstaff is unacceptable. It is unacceptable even if there is a major problem like the food being inedible or the order being incorrect altogether. These things can be fixed. And while it is unacceptable behavior, it is also an indication of a major character flaw in measuring leadership abilities.

Strong, successful leaders understand the concept of identifying with people regardless of their situational role. They present themselves in any and all situations as having an ability to recognize a person for their status as another human being worthy of respect regardless of position. These people practice courteous, polite, respectful treatment of others regardless of situation. Their actions reflect unconditional acceptance. They've learned that regardless of the situational circumstances, humans are equals and deserve common courtesy. They display empathy, an understanding of others, and have identified with *empathic leadership and humility* as a foundation of their approach to all people.

One individual who possessed such an empathetic, humble leadership skill set was a gentleman named Kevin Sullivan. Kevin at one point in his leadership career was the president of the Florida Restaurant Association after having managed and owned a top-tier restaurant, Dan Dowd's Steak House in Plantation, Florida. I never met Kevin Sullivan but did have the pleasure of working with his daughter Kristin Sullivan-Stoesser at one point in my career as we toiled together in the direct mail industry in the late 1990s. Kristin Sullivan-Stoesser, or "K Squared" as she is fondly referred to, is by far one of the most hyper, talkative, effervescent, intelligent people I know. She is a human dynamo with an energy level surpassed only by her drive and work ethic.

I was fortunate enough to catch up with Kristin recently as she answered my inquiry about exemplary leadership in action. Kristin is currently the vice president of advertiser solutions and sales at Comscore, a media measurement company based in Chicago. When I asked Kristin if she would be interested in providing an exemplary leadership case or two for this book, it didn't surprise me when she offered twenty-one of her own! She's always been the overachiever. In fact, several of the items offered in the bonus lesson of this book came directly from Kristin's input.

Yet most importantly, Kristin told me about her father Kevin and his influential, respectful leadership style. She told me about how as the oldest of nine children, Kevin was told that he wouldn't amount to much, that he was stupid and lazy. That his efforts weren't good enough. That he would never be successful. Those limitations were put on him by Kristin's grandmother, who did not realize that her eldest child suffered from dyslexia. Throughout most of his youth, Kevin struggled with a learning disorder that challenged his reading skill and comprehension.

Kevin Sullivan battled through an enormous personal challenge to find his way into the restaurant business later in life and

75

there overcame his dyslexia and worked his way up the corporate ladder. He learned about himself, and more importantly, he learned about other people. He learned to manage and lead, and he did this based on the simple principle of treating others with respect and dignity, keeping a level of humility in thought and action along the way.

As he managed his restaurant, he instilled in his staff that they too in kind would treat any and all with dignity and respect. He expected no less. He demanded a lot more. A situational value system was nonexistent. It didn't matter if you were the hostess, or on the waitstaff, or were one of the chefs, busboys, or cleanup crew. Everyone who worked in Kevin Sullivan's restaurant would be treated as a peer, as a coworker, as an individual working on a team. Everyone would be treated like a person wanted to be treated. Kristin personally experienced this premise numerous days and nights with her father and watched and learned firsthand what a servant leader actually does in the workplace. Although too young to wait tables, Kristin was old enough to make salads in the kitchen and was privy to the "before shift" waitstaff meetings held every night before dinner service. Those meetings covered policies, nightly specials, and introductions of new hires and were an opportunity for team-building conversation.

On one occasion one staff member asked Kristin, "Do you know how good a manager your father is?"

Kristin asked for more information of the fellow employee. "What do you mean? To me he's Dad, he will always be Dad first, so fill me in."

The fellow employee went on to tell Kristin that her dad had a policy at the restaurant that whenever one of the staff, regardless of position, had fallen on hard times and needed personal assistance, the staff would take up a collection for that person. As is true in many businesses, here when you don't work, you don't get paid, but in the restaurant business, a large part of a waitstaff's income is variable, based on tips. When a waitperson is unable to work their floor shift and loses their tip income, the personal challenges become even greater. This fluctuation in income opportunity can lead to an alarming staff turnover rate. Turnover reasons vary as many restaurant workers are in transition or going to school or just there to make ends meet until something better comes along. But whether it was illness or problems at home or individual challenges, Kevin Sullivan always offered to help anyone on his staff. The team would take up a collection, on a strictly volunteer basis, for the individual in need. There was no pressure to contribute. There was no retribution if you couldn't contribute at the time. You gave if you could—and *Kevin Sullivan would match out of his own pocket whatever the total contribution was for the individual.*

That is a classic example of leadership putting aside any thought of situational preference. That is a perfect example of a leader understanding how their actions and subsequent follow-up actions have an effect on their team. Very easily Kevin Sullivan could have ignored the latest employee in need and went about his own business. Instead, he made it a best practice to treat others as equals and lend a helping hand to people in need and took money out of his own pocket to back up that practice. He demonstrated respect for others regardless of circumstance or position.

Kevin Sullivan recognized that someday he may be in a position of need or maybe toward the end of his career would take on a lesser role in the restaurant industry or maybe even transfer to another career opportunity, perhaps with less stress or responsibility, as he entered his waning years. He realized that treating people with respect and dignity is a two-way street. He wanted others to view him as a person worthy of their respect and courtesy, so he himself treated people at all levels the way he wanted to be treated. He asked his employees to smile, look people in the eye, acknowledge them as another human being, be friendly, approach them with enthusiasm, say please and thank you, and above all "let them see how you thoroughly enjoy the opportunity to assist them in having a most pleasurable dining experience." Kevin Sullivan identified with this key element of leadership and exemplified it every day during the course of his restaurant responsibilities. He was the example of walk the walk and talk the talk as he treated each of his employees as peers, as equals, as friends, as partners, as family.

The "corporate ladder" is a relatively overused piece of business jargon, an example, a cliché, a synonym for promotion and additional responsibility. It is certainly easy to view the corporate ladder as one-sided, with the only way being up. The interpretation can be "keep going till you reach the top," as so many so-called leadership gurus preach to their flock of willing junior executives and midlevel managers. This thinking disregards the need to consider others and is merely focused on one's own success. There's not much mentioned about how to get there legitimately in humanistic terms. A path that is individualized and focused on personal accomplishments and disregards the contributions of others is a dark one indeed. True leaders know they are only able to be successful in their leadership role by having support, respect, loyalty, and appreciation from those they lead. And in order to earn this level of commitment, a true leader values the concept of being a respectful human being to others along the way, leading their business life much the same way they do their personal life.

The ladder goes both ways is a metaphor for life's sometimes harsh reality. It can also be the ultimate lesson in humility. If you've ever been at the top or near the top of an organization and subsequently have been metaphorically "knocked off" or taken out of your leadership role for whatever reason, you know the challenges of starting over. You can identify with having to accept your fate and the requirement to move on to land another opportunity. You may be reading this thinking, *Thank goodness I built a strong network, had great references, had excellent experience, and easily transitioned to another role.* But I hope you are reading and thinking that along with taking care of yourself on the rungs of the corporate ladder, you took the time to take care of others regardless of which rung they stood on. That you treated them with dignity and respect so as to nurture the empathic leadership in them along the way. These people may be the ones who provide a much-needed lift to restart your career. They are not to be taken for granted.

Kevin Sullivan exemplified a leader who never got the chance to experience the downside of the corporate ladder from a sense of changing roles or industries or positions in his waning years. Yet he will always be remembered by those he led, managed, guided, nurtured, assisted, and treated with respect, dignity, and courtesy and by those he treated as equals regardless of position. Most of all, Kevin will be remembered by those who loved him as family, whether actual or symbolic, and by those who loved his exemplary empathetic leadership style.

Unfortunately, Kevin was killed in an automobile accident in his late forties. His legacy lives on in his daughter Kristin Sullivan-Stoesser, who has her father to thank for her significantly strong and admirable leadership style, and whom I thank emphatically for contributing her thoughts to this lesson learned.

A little humility is most appreciated by others in climbing the rungs of the ladder and certainly contributes to one's peace of mind on the way back down.

Thank you, K Squared.

Humility: Freedom from pride or arrogance; the quality or state of being humble; having or showing a modest estimate of one's own importance

Leadership in Action: Nothing demonstrates a lesson in humility quite like a situation in which the copy machine is acting up. You realize you don't know how to fix it, or better not attempt to try to fix it for fear of making a bad situation worse, and can only hope your office assistant will once again come to your rescue—for the third time that day.

LESSON #8: THERE IS NO POWER IF THERE IS NO RESISTANCE

By David Pauldine

For good ideas and true innovation, you need human interaction, conflict, argument, debate.
—Margaret Heffernan

When speaking to professionals rather new to the executive ranks, I ask them to raise their hands if since making it to the top, they have noticed an increased level of resistance or push-back from their employee base. I clarify that this resistance can be active or passive—it's all the same. I'm looking to know if they can "feel" the increased levels of resistance coming from their employees, particularly as these leaders ascend in their organizations. All hands go up. Every time. Many then share that this can be frustrating and often "spoils the joy of being a leader." That's when I share this catchphrase "There is no power if there is no resistance."

Let's unpack this a bit. Imagine two arm-wrestlers, locked in and ready to go at it. Elbows are on the table, hands intertwined, and each just waiting for the horn to blow. The horn blows, and arm-wrestler #1 literally does nothing. He puts forth no effort, no resistance to his opponent. As a result arm-wrestler #2 quickly flattens his opponent, and the match is over. Certainly arm-wrestler #2 can declare that he won. He can say that he beat arm-wrestler #1. But can arm-wrestler #2 claim that he is the more powerful of the two competitors? The answer, of course, is no. The winner in this case will never know if he was power-dominant over his opponent because there was no resistance offered by that same opponent.

Now, picture yourself driving down the highway at sixty-five miles per hour. You roll down your window and stick your left arm straight out as you drive. Of course, this is not recommended, but stay with me here. You'll notice that the wind force makes it such that you have to exert some effort (power) to keep the arm steady and straight. If you don't use your strength to resist, the force of the wind will blow your arm backward and I imagine cause you some pain or even injury in the process. So, you generate the strength necessary to resist the wind force and as a result are able to hold your arm straight, thereby making you triumphant over the wind force. You have power over the wind. Now, imagine you are in your car in the driveway. The car is not running. You are simply sitting in an idle vehicle. Now once again, you lower the window and stick your arm out. Entirely different feeling, right? It's just an arm in quiet air. It takes no effort to hold your arm straight because the wind is putting up no resistance to your action. In this case, can you claim you have power over the air? No, I don't think so.

The point here is that if you get resistance, it means you have power, or authority. Let me point out that power in these examples is not meant to be pejorative. It's not meant to connote something we lust for to use against those with lesser strength. I'm referring to power with a small *p*. Sometimes when we hear the word "power," we think of it in evil terms. Think back to all those movies you've watched over the years where an evil protagonist looks into the camera and says something like: "Once I complete my dastardly act, I will have the power to rule the world!" Queue up the evil laugh now. No, in the context of this message, power here simply means authority or influence—and yes, leaders do have both.

When you encounter resistance by those you are leading, it means that you have arrived. It means you have some influence, some authority. It comes with the territory of being a leader. If you didn't have any authority (power), few would care enough to resist you. So, take it all in stride. The pushback you receive from time to time simply validates that you are in a position of some authority. Now, what you do with that authority will be the test of your leadership effectiveness. There are twenty-one chapters in the book you are now reading that will help you with that effort.

I used to tell my team that the biggest compliment they could pay me would be to disagree with me in front of others. When they did, it was important that I received their pushback with grace, that I did not "jump" the person voicing the opposing view, and that there were no repercussions for that person. Similarly, the person presenting the opposing point of view must do so in a respectful manner. Disagreeing with the boss is fine; disrespecting the boss is not. Of course, as the boss, I am free to accept the opposing idea or reject it, but what matters most is that there is the freedom to express it in the first place.

I've experienced how expressing a differing point of view than the boss—in front of others—can be liberating to the creativity and innovation of an enterprise. It sounds easy, but to many it is hard because the ego gets in the way. When those being led do not speak up, an organization becomes an autocracy. No doubt, the corporate graveyard is filled with examples of failed companies that operated as autocracies. By contrast, when leaders welcome pushback, good things happen. First and foremost, better decisions get made. No organization benefits when team members go along with the boss on a decision even though the team clearly had a better idea. Second, the leader that welcomes professional dissent will attract and retain the best talent.

Bringing this full circle, the message is that one cannot have power if there is no resistance. It is the resistance that we face on the job that allows us to demonstrate our measure of authority, our effectiveness, and yes, our power. When you encounter resistance on the job, relax. Realize that the resistance is a necessary component for leadership to emerge and for you as the leader to step into the light. From a more macro perspective, resistance keeps an organization from mediocrity. Resistance fosters continuous improvement. Resistance invites collaboration and consensus. Getting pushback strengthens the decision-making process of leaders and their organizations. Resistance will help kill a bad decision before it gets made. And that's an exceptionally good thing.

Sticking with a similar theme, let's change gears a bit.

Early in my career, I read an article in the *Harvard Business Review* that stuck with me for over thirty years and became in many ways an operating credo behind my leadership style. The premise of the article is that there are three responses to leadership: 1) rebellion, 2) creative individualism, 3) steadfast compliance. When you look at numbers 1 and 3, you get a quick idea what they are. Rebellion, of course, is when the inmates are running the prison. Needless to say, we can't *have* that. Steadfast compliance is a fancy way of saying the organization is filled with yes-people. And we don't *want* that. That takes us to creative individualism. This is when those being led understand that they must sign on to the organization's norms and values. That is nonnegotiable. However, after that, everything else is open to question.

About five years into my career, I took on a new assignment. It was a promotion to run a sales office. The position came open because my predecessor had been fired. We had eighteen sales representatives plus an office staff of five or six. The word around the company was that this office was a handful to manage. The personnel were ornery, demanding, and just plain hard to manage. I learned that my predecessor had taken a strong hand and ran things by mandate of the boss. I suspected this was contributing to the team "acting out." I arranged a meet and greet session with my new team on my first day in the job. I purposely set it up off-site so as to create a neutral environment. No one other than the team was invited. In my opening statement, I took the team through the *three responses to leadership.*

I emphasized I couldn't have rebellion and didn't want yes-people. We talked about creative individualism and how it could manifest in our day-to-day working together. At that meeting I learned that the sales team was edgy in part because they had worked six days a week for several months. The team had been told they had to work on Saturdays until the office had met its goals. This was in the era before wage and overtime laws came into effect. I could see that this was a major pain point—and understandably so. This mandate reminded me of that expression "The beatings will continue until morale improves."

I thanked the team for the feedback and told them that effective immediately, no one had to work Saturdays anymore. I told them that they were encouraged to take the day off and rest up, spend time with their families, and so on. And then I mentioned that they were not forbidden from working Saturdays, meaning, if someone wanted to, they could. I promised no judgment of any kind and that we would now begin to trust each other moving forward. In the beginning nearly everyone continued to work on Saturdays. The difference this time was that those who showed up on Saturdays were there because they wanted to, not because they had to. Over time more and more took Saturdays off, and things began to click. There were many times in that first year where I listened to the pushback coming from the team and adjusted the way we did things. Other times I listened but did not act. But the team always had a voice, and for that we were a better unit, pushing each other to better ourselves. The following year—year two of my managing the team—we were awarded the sales office of the year award amid an organization that had a dozen similar offices.

I came away from this two-year experience solidly behind the principles of the *three responses to leadership* and oriented future teams that I led to this overall philosophy. This mindset served me well in my career. I learned that no one wants to come to work and simply fall in line. The talented people in an organization want to change the world. They want to make the organization stronger, quicker in its execution, better at customer service, and so on. In short, they want to make a real difference. And to do so, they have to be allowed to pushback now and then. An organization that allows its good people to run, to question the status quo, to seek continuous improvement is an organization that will attract and retain top talent. More importantly, these organizations will achieve superior results. This is made possible by a leadership team that allows—and expects—creative individualism to exist and thrive within its workforce.

There is a cost when those being led do not offer pushback or resistance or similarly, when leaders react negatively or even retaliate against those that speak up. The 1986 spaceship *Challenger* disaster would likely have been averted if "all the president's men" had had the collective courage to inform Ronald Reagan of the problem identified with the spaceship's O rings. The problem was that nobody spoke up.

About ten years into my career, I worked for a man who truly was an autocrat. He didn't like to admit that someone below him on the org chart had a better idea. It was difficult for him, therefore, to accept input with poise. He would get snarly and typically find a way to dismiss the ideas I and others would give him. He would often revert back to a "my way or the highway" authoritarian stance possibly because he truly was uncomfortable being around those that were as bright as he—or brighter than he. It was no fun working for someone like this, and I left my job inside of a year under this manager. It really is true that people don't leave organizations; they leave their manager. The shame was that not only did his failure to welcome pushback cost him talent, but the organization just never got any traction. Over time organizations with those kinds of leaders become chock full of yes-people. The best and brightest won't opt in. When that happens mediocrity at best is all that can be expected.

In his book *Winning*, Jack Welch refers to the importance of candor in an organization. That's one way to look at this. As leaders we need to insist on candor at all levels of our organization. Without it, there will be a supreme lack of clarity, mistakes will increase, and opportunities will be lost.

There's a story about Nikita Kruschev that will further illustrate the point. Kruschev led the Soviet Union during much of the Cold War as the first secretary of the Communist Party from 1953 to 1964, and as chairman of the Soviet Union's council of ministers from 1958 to 1964. He served under Soviet dictator Joseph Stalin for years and was an intermediary between Stalin and his generals. He supported Stalin's purges and approved thousands of arrests. Under Stalin (and Kruschev), millions of people were executed or sent to the gulag labor camps. In 1960 Kruschev came to the United States and made a speech at the United Nations. At the end of his speech, media questions were entertained. At one point a member of the media asked Kruschev how he could justify all those years of Stalin's iron-fisted rule. The journalist asked about the executions, the crimes against humanity, the social injustice, and so forth. The questioner concluded by asking Kruschev what he personally was doing all that time while such evil things were taking place. Kruschev waited for the interpreter to translate the question. He then became red in the face and shouted out, "Who asked that question?" He did this because the camera lights were so strong that he could not see from where the question came. There was no reply. No one dared speak up. Kruschev shouted, "I say again, who asked that question?" Again, the room was silent. I imagine most of the journalists were looking down at their shoes. Kruschev then said, "I'll tell you what I was doing. I was doing what each of you are doing right now." Later it came out that Kruschev was not mad at the journalist who asked the question; he was mad at himself. He was mad that over all those years of evil actions taken against Soviet resisters, he never spoke up. He was mad that he didn't challenge his boss or at least attempt to dissuade him. He was mad because he did not try to make a difference, he did not influence things in a more humane direction.

Effective leaders let go of their egos and encourage those being led to challenge and even resist when warranted. In doing so, mistakes are averted, and the right calls get made. Over time these leaders build organizations that attract and retain top talent, engage in more innovation, drive toward continuous improvement, and more times than not, outperform their competitors.

> **Candor:** Unreserved, honest, or sincere expression; forthrightness.

> **Leadership in Action:** When you disagree with your boss and you privately let him know as such, he tells you that he appreciates your honest opinion and thanks you for speaking up and then asks you with whom else you've shared your opinion.

Don't worry, stay strong and realize it's just his way of being candid with you.

LESSON #9: LEADERSHIP AND CONFLICT

Successful leaders manage conflict; they don't shy away from it or suppress it but see it as an engine of creativity and innovation. The challenge for leaders is to develop structures and processes in which such conflicts can be orchestrated productively.
—Ronald Heifetz and Marty Linsky

Many thanks again to David Pauldine for his words of wisdom in the previous lesson learned, which provides me a perfect segue for what follows.

Have you ever met a person who enjoys conflict with others when it comes to making business decisions? They view the business decision-making process as a battle in which they have to win; they must defeat those who have an alternate solution or difference of opinion. Their solution or opinion is the only one that matters, and their action will validate their authority and superiority. They can't wait to get to the meeting, to spout about their solution, to let others know they are ready for a verbal fight and will do whatever is necessary to ensure they win the battle for strategic direction. They love a good fight, simply for the fight's sake.

How about a person who avoids conflict at all costs in similar circumstances? They view the business decision-making process as an opportunity to remove themselves from the process simply because there are others who have an alternative solution or a difference of opinion. They don't want to confront their antagonist even though their opinion and input is needed to make a decision. They would rather keep their thoughts to themselves than engage in a verbal struggle with those who disagree. They will conveniently miss the meeting, double-book themselves to attend another meeting, or not be available for whatever reason. They can't stand the person who loves to fight.

Better still, have you ever worked for a leader who exemplified either of those negative fight or flight characteristics?

If so, then you will appreciate this lesson learned with a sense of personal gratification.

Exemplary leaders are skilled conflict managers, willing to engage conflicted people to guide them to attain resolution for their own benefit and for the benefit of the organization.

Whether or not you have experienced a situation whereby members of leadership is at odds with each other, you most likely concur that the leader who works for the development of people and the betterment of the organization is the one who fully and effectively knows how to guide the opposing combatants through the resolution process. Conflict is a normal part of everyday business and can actually be healthy for the organization and its people. As long as it doesn't become so conflicting as to prevent the organization from continuing to move forward in its quest for continuous improvement and in making sound strategic decisions.

As effective leaders are likely to do, they know it is critical to separate the people and personalities from the problem in order to gain a true perspective on the situation. Their solution will be based on the issues at hand and not the people involved. Yet they also know part of their mission is to bring people together as an ultimate resolution to conflict. They will challenge those who fight and do the same with those who avoid, but they will do so in a manner that promotes resolution and collaboration while preventing further conflict between the conflicted parties. They are exemplary at demonstrating conflict resolution skills that are synonymous with appropriately leading people. Becoming an expert in conflict management is a mark of an effective leader, yet to reach a level of expertise in this critical area takes time, effort, and a willingness to learn from conflict experience.

Depending on the difficulty of the situation and the individuals involved, there are numerous categories of resolution skills that all leaders should be cognizant of and act on consistently to build their level of expertise. When faced with a situation of conflict, exemplary leaders engage, act, and seek resolution. They are focused on bringing people together, not apart for the benefit of the organization and for the individual development of those involved in the conflict.

They do not argue, avoid, assume, ignore, or provide an immediate answer to the conflict. They do not add fuel to the fire or exacerbate the situation. They do not choose sides or overreact emotionally.

> *Exemplary leaders learn, develop, and consistently use a superior level of people skills expertise and are naturally calm in their conflict management delivery.*

Throughout my career I have been fortunate to work with exceptional leaders who were experts in conflict management resolution. The following is a foundational list of conflict management resolution skills for your consideration and exploration. I have personally witnessed extraordinarily successful leaders actively engage in a multitude of these characteristics to dissolve issues that others with less experience or willingness may have been less successful in bringing to fruition.

Successful people-leaders master their ability to engage in these conflict management resolution skill sets by doing the following:

- **Disarm the threat**—when the threat is evident, disarm its influence on the situation and those involved by accepting the significance of the issue and by supporting a level of calm, cool, collective behavior. If the leader is calm and respectful, the expectation is the conflicting parties will follow suit.
- **Listen**—take the time to interview and allow the conflicting people the opportunity to state their case separately and without interruption. Do this in private if necessary; take appropriate notes to capture the details of the situation; especially listen for areas of common ground as well as difference of opinion to use as negotiating points for resolution.
- **Understand**—ensure as complete and detailed understanding of the situation as possible; take the time, recount thoughts, and give feedback on your understanding of the situation to the person just interviewed.
- **Demonstrate patience**—take the time to get to the bottom of the situation and not rush to a solution or decision; allow others to do the same. While we want to keep the process moving along, it is best for intelligent and beneficial conversation to occur when all parties are ready

to assume their level of responsibility to the organization. Set a timeline / deadline if necessary, and be clear about expectations.

- **Engage people**—separate the issue from the people, engage with the person spoken to as a confidant, ensure their trust and act in the best interests of the organization; assure them their position is taken into consideration for resolution.

- **Watch the nonverbal cues**—be cognizant of body language and facial expressions that may provide an indication of insecurity, uncomfortableness, or aggravation. Address those potential barriers with nonthreatening check-in questions, allow the other person to talk and address their issue in this regard.

- **Seek empathy**—rely on personal appeal to understand the situation from their point of view, do not assume or be influenced by your own perceptions, focus on their thoughts and especially their feelings regarding the situation, and do not prejudge.

- **Handle the emotions**—stay in control of emotions regardless of how volatile the situation may be or how aggravated or emotional the person interviewed is. Let them vent if needed. Be levelheaded and calm; be the voice of reason.

- **Keep organizational goals in mind**—the effort to resolve conflict must be in the best interests of the desired organizational outcome, the desired end result. The issue may be a difference in opinion as to how to achieve those goals, yet the leader's job is to stay on task according to the organizational goal and what it means to the organization when this goal is achieved.

- **Mediation**—leaders understand the importance of mediating a solution that allows both parties some semblance of satisfaction yet is also in support of the organizational goals and represents a legitimate resolution process for the situation. At times it may be best to have the people engaged in conflict assemble in a meeting, during which the leader provides an opportunity to clear the air, not to play judge and jury but to allow for open discussion to resolve the issue.

- **Collaborate**—it is evident in negotiations that a collaborative discussion and solution allows for all parties to feel a certain level of contribution to the solution and feel they have come out with a win-win scenario. The leader is the chief collaborator and sets the tone of willingness to engage ideas to reach a team solution on the issue and is the one who brings people together to grow and develop, to learn, to resolve.

- **Solution-oriented**—the leader sets the tone for the end results, is focused, and committed to delivering a solution to the conflict, and in this regard, establishes this tone throughout the meetings. The leader is intent on reaching an agreement that will provide benefit for all involved and protect the best interests of the organization.

- **Problem solve**—just as the leader is solution-oriented, they also love to problem solve and love to do this via the constituents. The leader knows how to engage constituents' thinking to reach a solution simply because the leader understands their perspective and uses that understanding to develop options to solve the problem.

- **Critical thinking skills**—exemplary leaders keep things simple yet have an uncanny ability to dig deeply into the situation to allow for full understanding of outcomes. The leader has the ability to analyze and evaluate complex subject matter and break down that information to guide, influence, and take appropriate action.

- **Stress management**—does it seem to you that people are more tightly wound now than ever before? The pandemic of 2020 certainly added to that level of stress. The leader is a person who prevails over stress and helps others in this regard. Life without stress is death. So there will always be stressful influences in our lives. The leader handles the stress and encourages others to do the same by providing an outlet to deal with stress.

- **Appreciate the opportunity to grow/develop**—use the situation as another learning experience even if it represents circumstances similar to those of a prior situation. The leader's experience and confidence grows and the ability to handle difficult situations becomes common-place. Ultimately the leader has done it before, will do it again, and is happy to add this experience to their reper-toire.

- **Take it with a grain of salt**—there is no need to get de-fensive or to overreact if the situation gets personal. Stay calm, stay cool, stay in control. Be viewed as the leader with a levelheaded approach to all scenarios.

- **Stay positive**—resentment, anger, retaliation, and retri-bution have absolutely no place in conflict resolution. Nor do they have any place in effective leadership. The lead-er's positive attitude to conflict resolution allows for the opportunity to forgive and forget, move on, stay focused on desired results, and reach a level of solitude. Venting is done in private. Others who engage in resentment, anger, retaliation, or retribution are not leadership material and are eventually removed from the organization.

- **Curb the ego**—this isn't about accolades for the leader; it is about doing the right thing to ensure stability within the team. The leader allows team members to take the glory and takes a humble approach to conflict resolution.

As I worked through the above bullet points, I was remind-ed of the importance of building relationships as not only a foundation for conflict management but as a foundation for effective leadership. If they make an effort to build prosperous relationships with coworkers, the leader has a much better chance to engage in successful conflict resolution when and if the need comes about. In fact, conflict itself may be avoided altogether if there is a strong bond and healthy relationship within the team as established by the leader. Although disagreement will occur, and as previously mentioned this can be healthy to encourage innovation and interest, harsh conflict may be minimized if there is a level of respect and mutual commitment to acceptance from the team.

> *While conflict will occur, it is the effective leader who proactively diffuses the level of conflict intensity allowed.*

For those individuals who love a fight for a fight's sake, and for those who avoid others because of personality clashes or would just rather skirt their responsibility to participate in the decision-making process because their personal antagonist is going to the meeting, keep this in mind next time you have a potential conflict on the horizon. Take a breath, clear your mind, relax. Be patient with yourself and with others. Take a fresh approach to what may be your standard operating procedure. Try something different. Try to be a little more accommodating, a little more approachable, a little more responsible. Your team is counting on your leadership.

Patience: Bearing pains or trials calmly or without complaint; steadfast despite opposition, difficulty, or adversity

Leadership in Action: To fully appreciate the value of patience, the leader needs to look no further than his own team of direct reports. Their ability to maintain a level of calm similar to being in the eye of a storm is something to be admired.

This is usually most visible when the leader is not around.

LESSON #10: BE DETERMINED, BE INFLUENTIAL

Our greatest weakness lies in giving up. The most certain way to succeed is always to try just one more time.
—Thomas Edison

Now that I am in my latter years, there is one form of exercise that doesn't sit well with me anymore: running. Or better said, casual jogging in the neighborhood. Jogging for exercise is not going to appear on my daily agenda any time soon, or any time at all for that matter. While the mind wants to jog, the body says, *No way. Slow down, old man, you paid your dues years ago and now it's time to settle into a slower paced reality.*

Yet it really bothers me some days to think that I can't run like I used to in my youth. All those years of playing ice hockey and then subsequently coaching hockey took some toll on my knees, but mostly it's just a matter of getting old and being overweight. I'm sure it's that way for quite a few people in my age group. So, we walk and do what we can to stay healthy.

With that in mind, it was with great interest that I read an article published on LinkedIn by my friend and former coworker Elise Awwad. Elise is the chief operating officer at DeVry University and without question is one of the most results-oriented people I know. She is an A-type personality who leads by example in getting things done. Most important, however, is Elise's innate ability to influence others to get things done.

The leadership expert Ken Blanchard says, "The key to successful leadership today is influence, not authority." Dwight Eisenhower once said, "Leadership is the art of getting someone else to do something you want done because he wants to do it." The ability to influence in a positive manner is a true measure of a successful leader. In my eyes both quotes from these distinguished gentlemen translate to influential actions on their part that prompt the appropriate response they seek.

Now I am not sure if Elise wrote her LinkedIn article with the intent to influence her friends, family, coworkers, or peers or just for the sake of anyone who would take the time to read her article. When I spoke to her recently we didn't talk about the intent of the article. We focused on the content—although once one reads it, it is easy to see how intent and content are intertwined. We focused on her story, her commitment, and her dedication to running, but in my mind, there is a definite purpose to her story.

Just a few years ago, in February 2017, while on a business trip in San Francisco, Elise was walking across a plaza with several of her associates and slipped on the wet pavement. She landed hard on her left ankle. Embarrassed that she had fallen, but no worse for wear, Elise tried to get up but couldn't. She could not put any weight on her left foot. Fortunately, her associates provided much-needed assistance and drove her to the nearest urgent care facility.

Elise always took pride in being an athlete and at that time was into running 5Ks and similar short races, along with playing golf and working out regularly at her neighborhood gym. Her reaction to falling and being injured was to be expected. *Shouldn't be anything too serious, probably just a bad sprain, should be back up and running in no time*, Elise thought. Or at least that's what she hoped.

When the X-rays from urgent care were reviewed and brought to her for diagnosis, she could only gasp at the severity of the situation. Elise the athlete had broken both her tibia and fibula in her left leg. In fact the fibula was completely shattered. This wasn't the news she had anticipated. This was devastating. Yet there it was as plain as an X-ray could possibly be. This was a major injury that would require surgery and months of rehabilitation to return her to her normal routine. Elise didn't think about running anymore; she thought about being able to walk again without assistance. I can only imagine the level of discouragement and frustration Elise felt.

Hobbled and forlorn, her left leg splintered and wrapped in a protective bubble, Elise boarded a plane and headed home to Chicago. Just a few days ago, she had walked under her own power onto the plane bound for San Francisco and now was being pushed in a wheelchair for the return flight. This was devastating both mentally and physically. Elise fought hard to keep her emotions in check, but the next piece of news provided an even greater challenge.

Elise arrived home to Chicago, and in order to allow for the initial swelling to subside, her surgery was scheduled for the following week. A complex surgery that ended up requiring multiple screws and a metal plate to rebuild her ankle. The surgeon told Elise that most likely she would not be running any lengthy races in the future. Her aspirations to run long distances at a fun but competitive level were over. She wouldn't be able to handle the physical grind required to compete. Her running days were over.

Fight the tears, be strong, I can handle this, Elise thought.

Four and a half months of physical therapy followed surgery. Due to the seriousness of her injury, Elise had to learn to walk again. The muscles in the damaged leg had atrophied to the extent that they looked as if they didn't exist. She had to endure excruciating session after session of therapy designed to challenge her physically to rebuild those muscles. Yet these sessions ended up challenging her mentally as well. She had numerous breakdowns. There were times where she thought she couldn't go on; she would just let it be and accept the consequences. But she didn't give up; she persevered. While she was humiliated to be in the position of asking for help with what used to be the simplest of tasks like driving a car or going grocery shopping, Elise wasn't going to give up. Elise was an independent, self-sustained woman. She wasn't used to asking for help, but in this case, she had to and with extreme hesitation was forced to comply. What Elise was used to, however, when faced with a challenge was being determined. She wasn't going to give in. Her level of determination was second to no one.

I'm a fighter, I'm not done, I've got this, Elise thought.

Four and a half months of painful therapy from March through mid-July 2017 included four consecutive weeks in a soft splint cast, followed by four consecutive weeks in a hard cast, followed by four consecutive weeks in a walking boot, the first two weeks of which she was not allowed to put any weight on her left foot, so crutches were required, followed by the second two weeks of only 50 percent weight on her left foot while walking with a single crutch.

During one of her therapy sessions, Elise was on the receiving end of a little bit of leadership influence. Much to her surprise, her therapist said to her, "You know with your determination, I think you can run long distances if you decide to do so in the future." Elise didn't take her therapist's comment as being a manipulative attempt to get her to work harder in therapy. On the contrary she interpreted her therapist's words as motivation. She accepted the challenge. She accepted the influence. Elise's therapist shared with her a similar positive attitude approach to challenges, so the message was aligned with her short-term recovery goals. She accepted a new sense of focus and set her sights on a long-term goal that would change her perspective regarding determination.

She would run in the Chicago Marathon. But not only run in the marathon—she would successfully complete the marathon.

The next two and a half years challenged Elise's determination to reach and accomplish her goal. A lesser person may have given up, given in. There were numerous opportunities to stray from the training regime and miss a planned workout. The chance to go out with friends after a week of work was commonplace prior to her injury, but now she had to forego those opportunities to stick with her training. Diet and exercise were the foundations of her thought process to succeed.

Stay with the program. Focus on the end result. The effort you make now will pay dividends in the future. People are watching.

Don't think I can do it? Here, hold my beer (or in her case, water).

Elise's dedication paid off. She was ready for race day October 13, 2019. All the training, therapy, dieting, physical and mental determination had positioned Elise for success to achieve her goal, but they had also provided something else she hadn't planned on. While Elise worked diligently in her regime to attain her goal, her actions did something special for many others as well. She completed the 26.2-mile Chicago Marathon in a little over five hours, much to the excitement of her family, friends, and coworkers. She demonstrated a significant strength of leadership in action. Elise found herself in a difficult situation, accepted the challenge, set a lofty goal, and was determined to see it through to a successful fruition.

Perhaps it was unintentional, but more likely, knowing Elise as I do, I believe she was fully aware that by achieving her goal and telling her story, this undertaking would have a major positive impact on her leadership team and coworkers. She ran the marathon for herself but also as an example for her peers, coworkers, and DeVry students. Elise believed that by accomplishing a comeback from a devastating injury as she did, she would be setting an example that hard work and determination are cornerstones for success regardless of the challenge at hand.

And she was right. Her inspirational story was well received and garnered numerous personal accolades. But more importantly, her story impacted others—family, friends, coworkers, and several complete strangers—encouraging them to accept their own personal challenges and work diligently to overcome them. Elise's example provided the perfect, much-needed stimulus-influence to motivate them in a positive direction. Her actions led them to be more focused and dedicated to seeing their challenges to successful fruition.

Elise led by example and was determined her leadership would have a positive impact on others.

This sort of leadership in action via overcoming a personal challenge and achieving a goal is relevant for business leaders faced with similar professional circumstances. Regardless of the uniqueness of the challenge, people in the company are watching the leader's response and subsequent actions to determine if the leader is worth following.

How often have you listened to a leader's response to a crisis only to question her actions, which don't seem to be aligned with her strategy? The determined leader knows that to be successful, she can't just tell people what to do. She has to get involved and show people that difficult situations can be overcome with exceptional effort and determination, provided the solution is practical and within reasonable expectations. The action-oriented leader knows her responsibility to set an example, be a role model, and own the strategy. Add your own cliché if you feel the need. Yet it rings true.

If the leader acts by example, the followers are much more likely to go along with the strategy.

The organization will watch the leader's actions to gauge those actions as they correlate to the organization and ultimately the leader's strategy. If actions and strategy are aligned, there is a good chance for harmony in mission, a better chance for success in execution, and certainly an even better chance that actions will have a positive effect on outcome. The age-old cliché "actions speak louder than words" is still relevant, still viable for effective leadership.

Elise offered these key bullet points as foundation for others on how to deal with and overcome their personal challenges. I embellished and added to the list.

- **Have a goal**—put it in writing, start with "to" and set a specific date "by."

  (Something like "To enter, run in, and complete the Chicago Marathon by 2022, for personal health and professional achievement.")

- **Dedicate the time**—commit to your goal with a focused daily effort.

  (Write out a routine, a plan, a schedule, and stick with the plan.)

- **Be disciplined**—reward yourself for being accountable; focus on the positive outcome of your discipline.

  (The plan provides for positive reinforcement when you achieve mini milestones along the way)

- **Lean on your support team**—you can always count on the support of those you trust to have your best interests in mind.

  (Don't go it alone; you will achieve what you believe with the help of others who are aligned with your efforts, allow them to help you be accountable.)

- **Turn off the negativity**—remove the haters and doubters from your game plan by associating with those who support your efforts.
(If faced with a doubter, leverage their negative words as motivation to succeed.)
- **Execute on your plan**—go "all in" with your effort, dedication, and commitment to your plan.
(Envision the end result of your efforts in a positive light and celebrate your success in implementing your plan).

Elise and I maintained our friendship over the years, but since we are no longer coworkers and haven't touched base as often as we both would have liked, I was unaware of her traumatic experience. I was surprised I hadn't heard about it from mutual friends, but I was not surprised by the outcome. Elise turned a personal traumatic situation into a living example of what great leaders do when faced with a seemingly insurmountable challenge. These leaders knuckle down, determine to succeed, write their plan, and properly execute on their plan. There is not much that can get in their way or prevent them from achieving their goal. Barriers are hurdled, crossroads passed, disconnects reconnected, all in a manner which exemplifies the leader's actions in support of executing the strategy. They are determined to make it work. They are determined to make it work for themselves and for the benefit of their organization. They are determined to influence people close to them, whether it be family, friends, coworkers, or peers. They are determined to achieve. They are determined to lead.

Thank you, Elise, for the opportunity to catch up and for sharing your story with me. Your determination in this example is a model and to be commended. It is certainly a story that has the potential to influence others to take on a challenging situation and overcome it via a solid effort and proper execution of a plan.

But most of all, it is the kind of story that hits home with nearly everyone who has some physical challenges that may prevent them from doing what they really want to do. Perhaps it will influence those people to get out of their office chair and hit the gym, the treadmill, the elliptical machine. Maybe it will have an impact on someone who needs to lose a few pounds and get back in shape. Maybe it will even influence an old guy to walk a little more often and add a little more distance in his routine. Maybe that old guy will jog a few steps in his walks as homage to your dedication and your leadership story.

I think this lesson learned will do just what you thought it would.

Oh, to be able to run again, or at least go for a jog.

Determination: Firm or fixed intention to achieve a desired end.

Leadership in Action: The leader displays their strongest sense of determination at times when execution is underdelivering relative to strategy. It's either time to pivot from the strategy or intensify the execution. Either way the leader is determined to figure out how to make it work.

After all, she's accountable for both.

LESSON #11: LEADERSHIP AND ETHICS

Ethics and oversight are what you eliminate
when you want absolute power.
—DaShanne Stokes

Have you ever been faced with an ethical dilemma? For clarity, let's define ethical dilemma as a challenge to solve a problem whereby the options presented as possible solutions all carry some form of baggage. None of the options presented are perfect solutions. None of the options are absolutely acceptable. None of the options are straightforward. All of the options present some form of challenge from an ethical perspective.

Here's a situation for your consideration.

Let's say you are the manager of a local discount tire chain and your sales lately are in steady decline. Competition in the market is heating up, and your facility is feeling the pressure. The consumer has an overabundant number of options from which to choose to get their next set of tires, and your place is viewed as just another one of those options. There is no singular differentiating factor other than price, which is a direct result of the consumer's desire to get a good deal on their replacement tires. Let's face it, your store is viewed as a commodity. Something good needs to happen to help you increase sales quickly, or you may be looking for a new job.

As you are mulling over your sales reports and thinking about your resume, one of your outside salespeople bursts into your office. "Boss, I got the contract, I got the contract!" Presented for your review is an agreement between your operation and the local bus company. It is an order for replacement tires on nearly half of their fleet. This is a godsend, a windfall, a miracle! Well done, salesperson, now our sales figures will show a huge improvement and things will at least be on the right track.

Except there's something just a little bit awry with the contract. The local bus company wants, and specifically names, a top-tier tire that meets their organization's specifications for safety standards as required by law. OK, no big deal; that's to be expected. They want, and your salesperson agreed, to a 15 percent discount from rate card since this is a bulk order. OK, also no big deal; it can still work in your profit structure, but it does eat into your personal bonus money opportunity and your salesperson's commission. But he is standing in front of you gloating and smiling ear to ear as if he knows something you don't. So far it's OK; you're willing to take a little hit in order to get the sale, so you continue your contract perusal.

Things are pretty ordinary until you read this: "If requested tires are not readily available to meet client's replacement schedule, vendor has the option to substitute an alternative tire brand still within admissible safety standards. Client will be advised of the substitution prior to installation."

No mention of price reduction for substituted tires. No mention of renegotiated rates if substituted tires are used. No mention of quality differential. No mention of a substitute brand by name. They have expectations that the substitute brand will be within admissible safety standards, will be a likely replacement for the requested brand, and are willing to pay at the already negotiated rate for the substituted tires. They are on a deadline and want their new tires pronto.

The salesperson is ecstatic. If you substitute a different tire that is more profitable for your company, both you and the salesperson make a little extra cash. In his eyes, this is an easy decision. He negotiated the contract and seized an opportunity. He knew all along what the outcome would be and shielded his thoughts from his new client.

You, on the other hand, are nauseated. Substituting a different tire helps you personally, and helps the store numbers, and helps the salesperson as far as making a little extra money but doesn't give the client what they want.

You need the sale. You have a majority of the client's requested brand tire in stock and can get the additional quantity from your company's warehouse. You can take the order at face value and call it a day. Except then your salesperson thinks you're an idiot for turning away a more profitable opportunity via the substitution. In fact, he's been in this situation before with another manager and is perfectly willing to go to the district manager to plead his case. You know the district manager is a driver of a profit-first management philosophy and stakes his reputation on the premise that without a profitable business, there is no business at all.

What do you do? Are you in a no-win situation? Are you willing to substitute tires to appease your salesperson and most likely avert a "discussion" with your district manager? Are you willing to compromise your own integrity to make a little bit more money via the substitution knowing you have the client's requested tires in stock and at your beckoned demand? Or are you willing to fill the client's order as written, make less money, and deal with your salesperson and district manager later?

Working on your resume doesn't seem like such a bad idea at this point.

You, my friend, are facing an ethical dilemma.

Some of you may be thinking the solution to the abovementioned hypothetical is really a no-brainer. After all, you are the manager and are paid to make tough decisions that at times may not appeal to all involved. You are paid to do the right thing and in so doing will be recognized and rewarded for your commitment to integrity and ethical best practices. You are accountable for your salesperson and will take the time to fully explain your decision and get him to understand the long-term benefit of fulfilling the client's order as written in order to build a relationship for future business. You will meet with your district manager and tout the great job your salesperson did in negotiating this contract and how he left the door open for future business in landing this client. Or you will fire the salesperson for not doing the right thing for his customer and then take over the bus contract yourself for the time being. Many options, many choices, many tests of a personal value system, and many possible outcomes.

Yet when presented with this very same hypothetical, nearly one third of the people I spoke with and asked what they would do in this situation chose to substitute the tires and take the short-term higher profits for the company, their retail outlet, and for themselves.

Hard to believe?

Not really. The pressure to perform in business is not without attendant temptation. In fact, situations of this order are common in the workplace and occur on a consistent basis. So much so, in fact, that many organizations conduct ethics training and require their leaders to adhere to an established code of conduct, thinking it is best to be proactive when it comes to protecting themselves and their employees.

> *By definition, ethics is the discipline dealing with what*
> *is good and bad, and with moral duty and obligation.*
> *Ethics is a theory or system of moral values.*

And while we can debate the latter reference to moral values and the personal interpretation of what is and isn't morally acceptable, I will draw a line in the sand and simply say there is no gray area when it comes to ethics. And, especially, there is no gray area when it comes to leadership ethics. Either you abide or you don't. Either you have ethics, or you don't. Either you recognize the difference between right and wrong or you choose to look the other way. While it is perfectly legal to turn right on red, it is not always the best option, especially if you are turning into an already established traffic flow. Just because it's legal doesn't make it the correct choice.

There is of course another side of the story, as many people would concur. You take a personal interpretative approach to the situational outcome based on what you believe to be ethical and unethical or morally correct. And in this regard you understand how much risk you are willing to absorb. You have the freedom to make your own choice, live by your standards, and are an adult who will live by your own rules. You don't need anyone telling you what is right and what is wrong because you believe the interpretation of those two options is highly debatable depending on the severity of the circumstances. You have a complete understanding of your moral responsibility and in essence live by your beliefs in this regard. You turn right on red weighing the risks but engage with the foundation that it is your personal choice to do so. It's legal, and it's your freedom of choice to act thus.

I have never seen an issue generate as much debate regarding moral responsibility being in conflict with personal freedom as the COVID-19 pandemic in 2020. To wear a mask or to not wear a mask? While I believe this question and its subsequent conflicting response scenarios became highly politicized, it is a classic example of the conflict that occurs due to different interpretations of moral values. What seemed a perfectly logical, scientifically based answer to the question for one group of people, or in this case more than half of the entire US population, was in direct conflict with the beliefs and pursuit of personal freedom for a little less than half of the country.

My point here is not to choose sides or say who was right or wrong, but to merely point out the differences in interpretation of and response to the question. Those in positions of leadership in the country certainly had a significant influence on each side's response to the question. Thereby a safe assumption would be that leadership in our country chose to interpret their response and subsequent actions based on their personal moral values, along with a consideration for public perception and political positioning.

In my own belief system, I adhere to the principle that abuse of personal freedom at the expense of others is morally irresponsible and ethically unacceptable.

I believe we develop our own personal moral value system based on influential individual experiences in each of our lives. I also believe the majority of our value system is ingrained in us in our early formative years yet can be influenced and changed as we develop and broaden our experiences. This influence can come to us in a variety of different ways via family, friends, work, religious affiliation, and education, to name a few.

So it was with great interest that I had an opportunity to speak with Neil Doughty, the director of BELIEF, the business ethics program in the college of business at my alma mater, Northern Illinois University. Founded in 2006, BELIEF is an acronym for Building Ethical Leaders using an Integrated Ethics Framework. Neil is in charge of a program that didn't exist when I attended NIU. BELIEF is a perfect example of a higher education institution taking a proactive approach to positively influence college students with the intent to guide them to develop into principled, ethical business leaders.

The need for a program of this nature is evident based on numerous examples of unethical and corrupt business practices instituted by people with weakened value systems in recent times. Kenneth Lay at Enron, Bernie Ebbers at WorldCom, and Dennis Kozlowski at Tyco are a few of the individuals who come to mind, infamous for their highly publicized ethics violations at their respective organizations.

The BELIEF program operates in four functional areas related to curriculum, faculty, students, and communication. BELIEF is supported by four different groups that drive the operations and activities of the program: faculty for ethics, corporate partners, alumni, and LEAD, an acronym for the student organization Leaders in Ethics and Academic Discipline.

While it was my pleasure to offer my time to Neil as a guest willing to be interviewed about my business experience and specifically my perspective on business ethics, I was equally interested to learn about BELIEF and the positive influence this program is having on NIU business students.

A commitment to including an element of business ethics is at the core of the intent of the College of Business courses. BELIEF sponsors guest speakers, conducts a BELIEF Week focused on business ethics, and provides an opportunity for students to get real-life experience via business ethics case competitions.

In doing a little research regarding the BELIEF program and in reading through the program's operating handbook, I was immediately struck by two impactful points as presented under the heading of "Why do I need to be aware of ethics?"

The answer to the question comes in two logical points:

- "There are many high-profile cases of unethical business behaviors and there will likely be more in the future."
- "Studies have shown that you will be confronted with ethical dilemmas much earlier in your career than you may think."

The handbook content points out how premise number one affects more than just the perpetrators of the unethical behavior. Other parties like shareholders, stakeholders, employees, customers, and coworkers or those caught in the wake of the actions of the culprits may end up suffering as well. The second point speaks directly to the individual student and reminds them of the fact that they alone are responsible for their ethical behavior and developing their leadership skills now.

It follows up these critical opening points with the most pertinent and impactful statements in the entire handbook, one which is the main point of this lesson learned chapter: "Not only does one have to know the right thing to do, [but] one must [also] have the moral fortitude to do it. The courage to *take action* in these situations is referred to as moral courage and is the key to being an ethical leader."

I know I am not plagiarizing because I am more than happy to give the authors of this professionally written *NIU Business Ethics Handbook** the appropriate citation and my gratitude. Thank you, Terry Bishop and Pam Smith, for creating this excellent ethics handbook.

I could not have written the chosen quotes from the handbook any more succinctly for the point I am trying to make in this lesson learned.

The importance of recognizing the right thing to do is clearly understood in ethical leadership but is truly engaged only when action in support of the right thing to do is taken. It is only truly engaged when leaders act.

---

* The BELIEF Program, *Ethics Handbook*, Building Ethical Leaders, Northern Illinois University College of Business, authors Terry Bishop and Pam Smith, 2011. © 2020 Northern Illinois University.

And by the same token, when knowing what the right thing to do is, and is understood and subsequently ignored via *inaction*, this choice of blindness is equally important. Both scenarios present the leader with an opportunity to impact the outcome, one in a positive manner and the other in a negative manner.

Leaders in effect must have the courage to act and the moral wherewithal to believe that their actions are in line with an outcome that provides a benefit for those involved. Their actions are perceived as in support of others and in support of the platforms that have a positive effect on the situations of others. In essence, their courage and their decision-making are aligned with consideration for others and not based on their own best interests. Although their own best interests may benefit, exemplary leaders make sound, strategic, and morally correct ethical business decisions based on understanding how the outcomes of those decisions affect other people.

I can only imagine what it must be like for the current business students at NIU to have this immense opportunity to learn these important leadership ethics principles at an early stage in their lives and certainly prior to being fully engaged in their business careers.

Perhaps some of those students were interns at companies or worked at organizations while attending school and have already been exposed to ethical dilemmas that tested their value system. Perhaps others have yet to experience a challenge in this regard, yet I can assure them their time will come. There may be others who have yet to realize the importance of the information that is available to them via the BELIEF program and will have to learn the value of ethics the hard way, much like I did.

The process of understanding ethics, ethical behavior, the associated consequences, and outcomes and applying that learning experience on a consistent basis only comes with being exposed to situations that test the parameters of learning. I applaud my alma mater for taking a proactive approach to preparing students for the ethical challenges that will undoubtedly face them in the business world.

I also applaud Neil Doughty for taking on the assignment of leading and directing this worthwhile program. His efforts to ensure that the BELIEF program is fundamentally dynamic, worthwhile, impactful, and most importantly influential in its effort to teach young adults the importance of ethical behavior and to conduct themselves in an ethical manner is to be commended.

Leadership comes in a variety of shapes and sizes, or in this case responsibilities and teachings, that will influence the next generation of leaders. Professors, teachers, administrators, and support staff are leaders in their own right as they represent leadership as role models, experts, mentors, and coaches. Their significant impact on their students is evident and will be verified in future years.

Congratulations, NIU College of Business and Neil Doughty, for demonstrating leadership in action. Your efforts are acknowledged and appreciated.

Integrity: Firm adherence to a code of especially moral or artistic values; incorruptibility.

Leadership in Action: There will be times when your integrity is challenged, questioned, and tested during the routine course of business. It is inevitable, regardless of how well you carry yourself or how well you conduct your business. There is always someone who wants to take down the leader.

When faced with an untrue accusation and forced to defend your integrity, keep this in mind: the person pointing a finger at you most likely has several fingers pointing right back at them.

Don't be afraid to fight for your honor because only you really know how defensible it is.

LESSON #12: ENTREPRENEURIAL LEADERSHIP

Do not stop thinking of life as an adventure.
You have no security unless you can live bravely,
excitingly, imaginatively, unless you can
choose a challenge instead of competence.
—Eleanor Roosevelt

By definition, an entrepreneur is a person who organizes and operates a business, taking on greater than normal financial risks in order to do so. In basic terms, an entrepreneur is an individual business owner responsible and accountable for the business's success or its failure. All strategic planning, decision-making, daily operation, process implementation and improvement, and financial responsibility for the continuation of the business lies squarely on the shoulders of the entrepreneurial business owner. "The buck stops here," as former President Harry S. Truman appropriately stated.

While the individual business owner assumes the risk, the owner also claims the rewards for their effort. Those rewards can be viewed in several different yet relatable categories, including profitability, professional recognition, community contribution, personal freedom, and sense of accomplishment, to name a few. Depending on the nature of the business, there could also be quite a bit of personal satisfaction gained in knowing the owner helped others achieve their goals, helped them reach their definition level of success, or helped them gain peace of mind or emotional, physical, mental, or spiritual well-being.

Therefore the true definition of an entrepreneur is a person willing to undertake a challenge having weighed the associated risks and visualized the potential rewards. The method by which the entrepreneur goes about building the business may be personalized to satisfy individual needs and specific goals. Yet regardless of risk, methodology, circumstances, or perceived outcomes, all entrepreneurs, much like organizational leaders, share a common characteristic.

> *Similar to leaders, who assume the responsibility and accountability for their organization's success or failure, the best entrepreneurs are passionate about owning their results. They love being in control of their own destiny.*

Their independence is a significant strength on which they build and one on which they conduct their business. They refuse to be categorized, marginalized, ostracized, or homogenized. They will not be "put into a box" or structured in their problem-solving abilities. They think freely, independently, and with the goal of nonconformity. They look for a better solution, a better process, a better method, a better way and are always challenging the status quo. They do not fear conflict but rather welcome it as an opportunity to explore options for partnership and collaborative resolution.

The entrepreneur's mindset is firmly established in the quest to do what's best for the customer while also operating ethically and within their established base of core values. They disregard negative influences and refuse to be swallowed up in red tape, corporate bureaucracy, or traditionalist thinking that prevents them from consistently moving forward with ideas and strategies that impact their business in the most positive manner.

They exude passion for their business and industry and are champions of the cause from a customer first standpoint. They use their business savvy to influence positive, impactful, and measurable consequential change throughout their organization. Their confidence is real and not to be mistaken for arrogance as they are perfectly able to support their bold direction with evidence-based facts and examples. They have a plan, a network, a following, and a commitment to relentlessly pursue their personal mission with a never-give-up attitude.

In fact, the best and most successful entrepreneurs are their own best leaders.

They are self-starters who actively engage in exploration committed to guiding positive change. This change is designed to disrupt a myopic viewpoint that plagues organizations and places people into a dismal state of comatose complacency. Their passion in this regard is complemented by their ingenuity, creativity, and enthusiastic desire to break the mold. They want—better still, *they need*—to be involved.

They need to act. Acting with purpose is in their DNA.

The similarities between leadership and entrepreneurship are evident. Great leaders and great entrepreneurs share a commitment to acting with purpose yet do so with calculated and acceptable risk, balancing the potential reward with the desired outcome.

And they do so with a limited fear of failure. They have their fear under control. Successful entrepreneurs and successful leaders relish in Tom Hopkins's famous words "Do what you fear most, and you overcome your fear." Successful entrepreneurs, much like successful leaders, realize there will be times when fear of failure or fear of taking a risk is inevitable, yet they also understand that they won't let their fears prevent them from accepting a challenge and working diligently to meet that challenge.

One such entrepreneurial leader who embraces this premise is my friend the highly regarded business executive and personal life coach Chris Yonker. In order to provide you with an accurate description of Chris, what his business influence embodies, his public persona, and his entrepreneurial philosophy, allow me the opportunity to take you back a few years.

I first met Chris Yonker in the early 1990s as he was a new sales hire with the 3M Company's national advertising division during the time I was the training manager for the same division. Chris attended my three-session sales training class, which was spread out over the course of a five-week period, whereby I would methodically and systematically place individuals in the 3M "box." They would enter the course as unmolded, unshaped, unpolished salespeople, and my job was to mold, shape, polish, and train them in the 3M way. The 3M way was the only way. They would leave the training session having gone through the most regimented, disciplined, structured, and scripted approach to sales training that a salesperson could possibly imagine. They would like it and be better off for it, and of course they would then be committed to the 3M mother ship. They would be assimilated. They would be 3Mers for life.

Only Chris was a little bit different type of student in a way that I had only seen once before, when Andrea McGinty graced my training class. Andrea later became the founder of It's Just Lunch, the world-renowned dating service. I didn't know it at the time, but Andrea was bound for bigger and better things as a successful entrepreneur in her own right. I should have recognized it then, but most likely chose to look the other way when Andrea would step out of class for long periods of time. I am sure she was bored stiff with the regimen and the delivery and had a much bigger game plan in mind for her undertaking.

While Chris was tolerant of the structure and regimen, and respectful of me doing my job, he had a remarkably similar restlessness about him to that of Andrea. He was different from the score of sales candidates that had passed through my training classes. He challenged me with a keen intellect, always asking questions that left others, and definitely me, pondering, "Why didn't I think of that?" He was bold but careful, brash but discreet, inquisitive, curious, and provocative in his approach to the subject matter and in his interactions with his classmates. He was not only different, but it was also evident he was smarter than the rest of us.

But he never showcased his intelligence to belittle any of us. His ability to stay within the parameters of the structure while most likely wanting nothing more than to get out on his own and actually experience sales allowed us to improve our classroom experience. I know it helped me become a better trainer at that time.

So it didn't surprise me that when I caught up with Chris nearly thirty years later, his entrepreneurial spirit had provided him with an opportunity to be an extraordinarily successful business consultant and life coach. His website, ChrisYonker.com, describes him as a vision alchemist, speaker, and author and as a world-leading expert in helping people to consciously navigate life's transitions. His focus is in ensuring high achievers and executives expand their consciousness and capacity for fulfillment. His efforts allow his clients to get clarity on what they really want, and he then guides them to make the strategy mindset and behavior shifts to get them there.

What did surprise me about Chris is that he had built his remarkably successful business while working full-time for 3M. (For those of us who live in a regular routine box, how is this possible? How can you operate a "side hustle" that demands the time and effort required to make it successful while still managing a territory and customer book of business for a Fortune 500 company? Especially a Fortune 500 company that is structured like 3M. Don't you have to choose between working for yourself or working for someone else?)

During this time he wrote a book entitled *Soul Intention: An Executives Guide to Building a Life by Choice, Not by Chance*. Oh, and he also launched a successful podcast entitled *Secret Thoughts of CEOs*, on which I had the pleasure of being a guest to converse with Chris about sales, sales management, and leadership.

Obviously, Chris figured out the secret to balance between a structured, demanding sales career and exploring a passion for operating his own business. And while he has several assistants to help him with administrative tasks and allow him the opportunity to focus his efforts on critical areas of importance, Chris basically determined years ago that he would be in control of his own destiny. He didn't let his fears stop him from being the successful entrepreneur he knew he would someday become.

Like many of us working for 3M back in the 1990s, we were pretty much ingrained in the commitment to "work for somebody." The income was good, the benefits were excellent, and the stability, long-term outlook, and security were to be appreciated. This was great until 1997, when 3M decided to sell the division where we worked. This meant either find another position within 3M or leave the company. It was an absolutely scary experience for me since I had been with the company I called home for nearly seventeen years. Although I was offered and accepted another position within 3M, it wasn't the right fit for me, so I ended up leaving a few months later for other opportunities. Perhaps not the wisest choice, but it seemed like the right move at the time.

I asked Chris about his personal experience with the division sale and if he went through the same sense of fear with which I had to deal. Chris told me he did think about losing his job, income, stability, and whether or not he would even be allowed to interview with other divisions of 3M. But he also told me something that helped me understand how he survived the ordeal. He realized that he could not let fear become the cage that locked him away and prevented him from attaining his goals. He wasn't going to let fear prevent him from getting to where he wanted to be. He would use this as a stimulus motivation to accept the situation, advance his career, and get himself in a better position in the long run.

While Chris managed to land a position with another division of 3M, it wasn't an easy transition. He had to move, was making less money, and had to uproot his family at the same time. Yet once again, Chris focused on the long run and refused to let his fears prevent him from getting him to where he wanted to be. He knew that in order to reach his level of defined success, his focus needed to be on what he wanted to move toward, not on what he wanted to get away from. His entrepreneurial spirit demanded that he commit to a future, not a past.

Throughout the course of the next twenty-plus years, Chris operated his 3M sales territory with much of the same entrepreneurial spirit. He questioned regimented tactics and demanded the freedom to manage his book of business with the customer's bests interests in mind while still protecting the 3M profitability. He spoke up, challenged the status quo, encouraged others to think for themselves, and developed a level of trust with his customers that allowed him to be recognized for his highly effective skill set. So much so that he coached other salespeople to break from their regimented, structured approach and to align their thought process with the customer's interests. He encouraged entrepreneurial leadership, the concept of being innovative, taking a fresh approach, empowering others to think for themselves, and developing their own sense of credibility in their customers' eyes.

Chris's story rings true from the standpoint of a managerial skill set as well. Chris told me there were managers to whom he reported who never could quite grasp the methodology by which Chris went about his business. They wanted him to be more aligned with their thinking, their structure, their philosophy. They wanted Chris's results as he overachieved expectations *every* year, and was frequently in the top 25 percent of sales results in the entire country. But they wanted the results delivered in the manner they thought was the correct way, their way, the 3M way. They were locked in the mindset of Chris needing to conform to their way of thinking. I think they were shortsighted, stubborn people who lacked imagination and creativity and were even envious of Chris's skill set. Chris was not afraid to rock the boat and refused to take their path to conformity.

Needless to say, Chris had his challenges with this type of manager-leader. He didn't get along with them and certainly didn't respect their thought process. They refused to recognize Chris as a free spirit entrepreneur fully capable of delivering the sales results albeit via his own methods while still operating ethically and professionally. Chris was subjected to several complaints from coworkers and a few managers regarding his side business throughout his 3M career, yet those complaints had little impact on Chris's results and far less on his commitment to his clients. Management knew of his side business and regularly reviewed his accounts to ensure there was no conflict of interest.

Chris operated with complete integrity and was open about his interests. He didn't hide anything.

The best manager-leaders that Chris worked with during his time at 3M were those that empowered him to do his thing, get the job done, keep the customers happy, help 3M be profitable, and at the same time allowed him to use his advanced skill set to help coach other salespeople to improve their performance. He challenged people to think, a well-established entrepreneurial leadership characteristic.

Chris used his strength as an entrepreneurial leader to focus on long-term strategy while still maintaining short-term sales outcomes. He formed relationships with his customers and guided them to improve their business while building and improving his own business at the same time. He maintained a vision for where he wanted to get to and executed on his strategy to get there.

When I asked Chris about how important it was to build relationships along the way in establishing his credibility and what he expected of his manager-leader, he answered largely along the lines of what I had anticipated. Chris's expectations of a leader are categorized into three simple yet profound areas.

- **Personal and organizational values are aligned**—working for the best interests of customers in an ethical and realistic manner while upholding integrity and organizational image.
- **Care about me**—someone who is interested in who I am

as a person, not just what I can do for the profitability of the organization.

- **Trust**—develop a relationship whereby there is never doubt regarding intent and respect.

Too often poor leaders and their associates engage in what Chris referred to as artificial harmony. Both sides fail to live up to or act upon the three principles that Chris offered. Both sides engage in lip service in these areas when in each other's presence but behind closed doors have a totally different perspective and direction. Violation of any of the three principles breaks the expected bond and prevents the leader and associate from realistically working together. It is hard to recover from a misstep in any of the three areas.

At the time of this writing, Chris had just left his 3M career behind after twenty-eight years. He is solely focused on his "side hustle" with expectations his business will continue to grow exponentially now that he can focus his efforts in this area 100 percent of the time. And while it is still hard for me to believe he worked for someone other than himself for a long time while building his own business part-time, it is relatively easy for me to believe how Chris maintained his direction to become as successful as he is. He has the entrepreneurial leadership platform down to a science. He chose to live life as an adventure. He chose to live it bravely, excitingly, and imaginatively. He chose a challenge instead of just being competent. He chose wisely.

Fortitude: Strength of mind that enables a person to encounter danger or bear pain or adversity with courage

Leadership in Action: A leader once told me she prays for fortitude every day, and sometimes twice a day. Those extra requests are usually prompted when the quarterly results are posted, and the stakeholders call is on the horizon.

And this comes from a person who owns her own company.

LESSON #13: I HAVE YOUR BACK

If the world attacks and you slide off track,
remember one fact, I got your back.
—Will Smith

There is a statement in my first book, *21 Lessons Learned in Sales Management*, which reads, "The only back he protects and covers for is his own." That statement appears in the chapter entitled "Leave Your Ego at the Door" and is in direct reference to my experience working with a person who was a master at covering for himself. He did nothing to protect the best interests of his team or for that matter, his coworkers. He was focused solely on his own best interests and could never get past his desire for self-preservation. His ego consistently got in the way of sound decision-making. If things went well, it was because of him, at least in his own mind. If things weren't going so well, it was because of someone else. His lack of accountability for the efforts of his team were evident and consistently hurt the morale of those who were subjected to his weak managerial attempt. To this day

I still question how he ever got into a managerial position. He exemplified poor leadership.

But most important for the topic of this lesson learned was this person's casual approach to caring for his coworkers. He never engaged in actually trying to build a personal relationship with us. Nor did he ever attempt to show any empathy for us personally. He treated us as commodities and would only associate with us in a rigid business setting. Perhaps he was too afraid to get close to us, or he didn't know the benefit of camaraderie in the quest to being a good leader. Or maybe he just didn't care.

The names are spared to protect those involved and because this lesson learned is certainly not about his poor leadership style. It is about a strong premise that contributes to a great leadership style. It is focused on an example offered by a person who knows firsthand what it's like for leadership to understand, empathize, and provide support in a difficult personal situation.

I met Dr. Linda Hoopes via LinkedIn as her background and mine have some similarities and thought she would be a great contact to add to my business network. She previously worked in higher education enrollment management—admissions for Mounds Park Academy, Upper Iowa University, and Waldorf University—and is currently the vice president of university partnerships for Ruffalo Noel Levitz (RNL). RNL has a longstanding reputation in higher education and is the result of a merger several years ago between Ruffalo-CODY and Noel-Levitz. Based in Cedar Rapids, Iowa, RNL is a specialist organization in technology-enabled services, software, and consulting for higher education enrollment management and fundraising. Their student satisfaction surveys and their enrollment services are a staple in higher education as evidenced by thousands of colleges' and universities' use of their services. They are a large nationwide organization with a long history.

Yet the story that Linda offered provided me with the thought that while large in stature across many spectrums and landscapes, RNL has a culture of a small family-run enterprise in that leadership allows itself to engage in helping, guiding, caring, and protecting its employees. At least this is true from Linda's perspective, and her opinion on the matter is founded in her personal experience with RNL. Mostly this opinion is based on how she was treated as an employee during perhaps the most difficult time in her life.

Linda was diagnosed with stage-three breast cancer several years ago and as she was a single mom going through transitions in her life, this news was not only unexpected but was also devastating emotionally, mentally, and physically. Linda didn't smoke, didn't drink alcohol, exercised regularly, and was in relatively good shape. But just ten days after having a routine mammogram, she was receiving chemotherapy and questioning whether she was going to live.

One can only imagine the stressful and negative thoughts that may go through a person's mind when a diagnosis this critical is presented. "Shocked" is putting it mildly. Linda feared for her life, yet thoughts about providing for her ninth-grade son raced through her head. What would happen to him if she didn't survive? Then there was the question of her keeping her job if she did survive. How long would she need to be away from work? Would they still protect her job? FMLA laws withstanding, would she still be seen with the same regard as prior to her diagnosis? "I can't worry about the job; I have to worry about surviving. I have to get healthy first; that's the most important thing of all. Why did this happen?"

Linda spent many tearful days and nights going through her treatment. Chemotherapy took her hair, her pride, her self-esteem, and temporarily delayed her career. But it didn't take away her dignity. It didn't take away her determination to survive. It didn't take away her fight for life. It gave her a new sense of being, one that was enhanced by the treatment she received from the senior leadership at RNL.

Unfortunately, cancer devastates far too many people in our society, and Linda could have become just another human resources statistic in a large company. Fortunately, that wasn't the case for her. The support she received throughout her grueling process of recovery was, in her words, "unimaginable." Linda did not realize the extent to which the senior leadership at her company would go to assist a fellow employee until she actually experienced it for herself. Throughout the course of her treatment and time off from work, Linda received meals from RNL, along with house cleaning services on a regular basis. Who does that?

Linda had to drive two hours one way for radiation treatments. She received assistance to ensure her travels were safe and transportation was reliable. Posttreatment she received a full spa day from RNL as a token of appreciation for her courage in fighting her disease.

But most importantly to Linda was the personal touch. Senior leaders from RNL visited her on a regular basis at her house. Linda learned they actually cared. As senior leaders they walked their walk and talked their talk and supported her as a person, not just as an employee. She was the recipient of that personal approach, that caring, that warm embrace from business associates who were more than just work acquaintances; they proved they were family.

The family-first culture established by the leaders at RNL is only as prevalent as the leaders who exemplify and demonstrate that culture to its utmost. For what good is a culture of words if it is not followed up with meaningful actions? Leadership at RNL demonstrated their complete understanding of the importance of caring for people not only because it is the right thing to do among fellow human beings but also because of the message it sends to the rest of the organization. Excellent leadership exemplified is knowing the value of taking care of people at their worst, most devastating times. Excellent leadership exemplified in these most challenging personal situations is focused on taking appropriate action for the individual while remaining cognizant of the outward appearance of those actions as a representation of the organization. Do the leaders demonstrate via their actions a belief in their mission statement and core values? Are they really people-oriented, people first, results through people, as it states in the company value statement, or are these words merely an exercise in rhetoric that carry little to no value when the chips are really down?

Great leaders engage with their people regardless of their position in the organization and are the ones who make the concept of "I have your back" real. This statement does not just apply to times when a fellow employee makes an error in judgment or the team's performance results do not meet expectations. The exemplary leader knows he or she is accountable for the challenges facing the team and is liable for the results. When things are going bad, it is the leader who steps up to accept accountability and determines a better strategy to improve results. When times are good, it is the leader who gives credit to the teammates for their contribution and results. Together they win.

Exemplary leaders strive to build a work culture whereby people feel good about their opportunities and about themselves. All of us have issues, challenges, problems in our personal lives. Leaders recognize this reality and choose to provide a level of support that places the employees' best interests at heart, knowing those actions will reap future benefit for all associated.

The principle of "I have your back" is founded in empathy. It is not just about covering for someone on the team when they make a mistake. That is the definition of the principle in its most literal and simplest terms.

> *The true measure of leadership in having a teammate's back is to fully understand their situation without actually having experienced that situation oneself.*

Sincere empathy is best displayed by actions that have a positive impact on the person, the team, and the organization. True leaders understand how powerful this type of action is in their ability to build a culture of respect and dignity. But they also understand how important this premise is to their own success.

Linda Hoopes certainly experienced this level of leadership and carries that example with her daily. Linda is a living example of courage as she battled her disease and is also a living example of loyalty when one is treated with compassion, care, and empathy. Linda is proud of her fight and her outcome. She's equally proud of her RNL leadership team, and with good reason.

They had her back the whole time.

> **Empathy:** The action of understanding, being aware of, being sensitive to, and vicariously experiencing the feelings, thoughts, and experience of another of either the past or present without having the feelings, thoughts, and experience fully communicated in an objectively explicit manner.

Leadership in Action: Empathy is at its best when the technology in your presentation fails miserably, prompting your boss to smile and congratulate you for perfectly demonstrating his skill set.

He knows he couldn't have done it any better.

LESSON #14: BE A GREAT TEAMMATE

*"Relationships and building solid ones are
the foundation of any great team."*
—Tony LaRussa

It is a challenge for me to write about being a great teammate
without relating this lesson learned chapter to some form of
sport, as in the sports arena there is often strong emphasis on
teamwork and team success. So if you are not a sports enthusiast,
please bear with me for a few paragraphs. The leadership lesson
learned will be evident to you later in the chapter when I change
gears from baseball to accounting. An interesting stretch, don't
you think? Read on.

The 1927 New York Yankees are considered by many baseball
aficionados to be the greatest professional baseball team of all
time. Upon review, it is easy to understand why this team is worthy of that recognition. Commonly referred to as "Murderer's
Row," a nickname earned by their reputation for having a fear-
some batting order that consistently knocked the cover off the

baseball and "killed" opposing pitchers, the Yankees were without question Major League Baseball's best team at the time. While that nickname certainly would not fly in today's culture, it was acceptable back then, and the Yankees lived true to their baseball reputation throughout the season.

The Yankees compiled a 110-win, 44-loss season, calculating to a .714 winning percentage, which is still the eighth highest winning percentage in the history of Major League Baseball. The 110-win season held up as a Yankee team record for 71 years only to be surpassed in 1998. The 1927 Yankees ranked first in all of the major statistical offensive categories that year, team batting average (BA), home runs (HR), runs batted in (RBI), slugging percentage (SLG), and runs scored (RS), and went on to win the World Series Championship in a sweep of the Pittsburgh Pirates 4 games to 0.

There were 7 future Hall of Fame inductees on this Yankees team, led by George Herman "Babe" Ruth, the greatest of all Yankees, who batted .356 BA with 164 RBI, 60 HR, and held a .722 slugging percentage (slugging percentage is defined as total bases divided by the number of at bats). He was actually bested in several categories by the American League Most Valuable Player award winner and Yankee teammate Lou Gehrig, who batted .373 BA, with 173 RBI, 47 HR, and a .765 slugging percentage. (For those non–sports enthusiast readers, these individual statistics are absolutely phenomenal and ones of which today's modern ballplayers would be envious.)

Without going into additional statistics, believe me, this Yankee team was comprised of numerous all-star contributors who achieved greatness and team success via their own individual performances. Yet it was best said by their historically agreed-upon and highly acclaimed individual star player, someone synonymous with the Yankees and a public facing leader who summarized the importance of teamwork in the following two sentences: *"The way a team plays as a whole determines its success. You may have the greatest bunch of individual stars in the world, but if they don't play together, the club won't be worth a dime."*

Babe Ruth's classic quotation provides a foundation on which all leaders should build when it comes to understanding the relationship between great leadership and great teammates. There is no one person who is greater than the team itself, and the success of the team depends upon the interaction of individuals working together to achieve a common goal. Therefore, if we try to distill the core meaning here, it is the leader of the team who provides the example as the ultimate teammate for the overall benefit of the team.

- No one really ever wants to be on a bad team, right?
- Do you ever hear anyone say, "I love to lose; I hate winning"?
- Bad team motto: "Losing is easy; there's no pressure to perform"
- Good team motto: "Winning is hard; we perform best when challenged"

Teammate defined: *Someone who cares more about helping a group or team to succeed than about his or her individual success.*

Taking that definition one step further, I offer that a leader not only cares more about helping others succeed than about individual accolades but also understands the importance of being a great teammate and displays this understanding via their individual actions. They set the pace, the tone, the example via their actions. And they do this without question 100 percent of the time. They know their actions influence the members of the team and are cognizant of their interactions with the team so as to legitimize their willingness to serve and help others. They are the best of teammates, and they demonstrate this recognition always—not some of the time, not when they feel like it, not when they want to, but always, regardless of circumstances.

If we were to ask sports, business, or executive coaches to provide a list of characteristics that exemplify great teammates and compare that to a list of characteristics that define great leaders, the similarity between lists would be evident but not unexpected.

Great teammates and great leaders exemplify these characteristics among others:

- **Selfless**—concerned more with the needs and wishes of others than with their own; they are unselfish
- **Humble**—show a modest or low estimate of their own importance
- **Sincere**—free from pretense or deceit
- **Inspirational**—influence others by their words and ac-

tions and provide a positive stimulus for motivation

- **High expectations**—engaged in doing things in a correct and accurate way; they expect to achieve their goals
- **Innovative**—introduce new ideas and encourage original and creative thinking
- **Optimistic**—hopeful and confident about the future, maintain a positive attitude regardless of challenges
- **Collaborative**—work jointly on an activity, especially to produce or create something
- **Self-motivated**—achieve because of their own enthusiasm or interest without needing pressure from others
- **Passionate**—show strong feelings or a strong belief in their efforts
- **Relationships**—connect with people and build upon that connection in a fruitful manner
- **Play any role**—get involved and are willing to accept any responsibility
- **Work hard to improve**—always making the effort to get better
- **Competitive**—love to get in the action and do so in a positive, professional manner; they love to win and will do so with respect for their competitors
- **Lead by example**—actions are in the best interests of their teammates and are based on doing the right thing at all times
- **Always come prepared**—they are students of informa-

tion and education, ready for the challenge
- **Understand their strengths and weaknesses**—self-aware of their ability and opportunities and work within their own capacity while seeking to improve
- **Positive body language**—focused and committed to carrying themselves in a well-respected manner
- **Hold themselves accountable**—responsible for their actions, accepting of results of their performance
- **Do extra work**—put in the time and effort
- **Always give 100 percent**—always give it their best effort at all times; they don't call it in; they don't "bag it"
- **Sense of humor**—easy to get along with; they joke about their own shortcomings
- **Coach in the making**—deliver praise in public and critique in private
- **Approachable**—accept feedback and are easy to talk to regardless of the difficult level of conversation
- **Support others**—look out for teammates and are proactive to assist
- **No blame, no excuse mentality**—take realistic responsibility for results
- **Reliable, honest, trustworthy**—exemplify integrity, reliability, credibility always
- **Respect themselves and others**—embrace a healthy self-esteem and guide others in this area
- **Offer encouragement**—helpful, supportive, compli-

mentary
- **Role model**—set a positive example for others to emulate

As we review this list of characteristics associated with being a great teammate, we see that the correlation between being a great teammate and being a great leader is evident and intertwined with many characteristics that provide a foundation for great leadership. We could add more of the big picture type of characteristics to the leadership side of the equation, such as visionary, critical thinker, strategic, and so on, but the crux of the point here is that successful leaders understand the foundational principle of quality people skill characteristics. And they demonstrate those characteristics on a consistent and routine basis. They are in effect demonstrating the similar characteristics of being a great teammate.

Thereby I offer the following premise: *Not all leadership roles are filled by great leaders, but those who care and are self-aware, strive to be great teammates in their quest to be great leaders.*

Let that sink in for a minute.

There is a significant and impactful correlation between being a great teammate and being a great leader. It is one built on respect for the relationship between the leader and the team, and vice versa.

My friend Andy Titen told me a story about a time early in his career when he experienced a teachable moment that underscored this valuable life lesson. Andy had just started in a senior accounting position, and one of his responsibilities was to review his new firm's prior year tax returns. Andy thought this would be a good idea to not only get a feel for the in-depth financial side of things but also a way to make a good impression on his new boss. However, when he requested the opportunity to review the prior year's returns, Andy's boss told him it wouldn't be necessary as he had previously reviewed the returns and the returns were compiled by an outside certified public accountant (CPA) firm. Andy's new company had been using this outside CPA firm for some time, and there had never been any issues with the company's returns.

Andy's boss told him it wasn't necessary but gave him the freedom to conduct a review if he thought it would help him become better acquainted with the business. So Andy pursued the opportunity and much to his surprise found a large unused tax credit that was not carried forward, which if implemented would have reduced the company's tax burden.

When he brought this discrepancy to his boss's attention, Andy was told he was probably missing something but that the boss would bring it to the CPA firm's attention. Upon doing so and after the CPA firm had time to review Andy's findings, the CPA firm openly admitted to making a mistake. The unused tax credit should have been carried forward to reduce the company's tax burden for the current tax year. The CPA firm indicated they would be filing an amended return to rectify the error.

Now just think about what transpired in this scenario. New employee reviews the work of an outside firm that had already been reviewed and signed off on by the boss. New employee uncovers a huge mistake that cost the company a large amount of money. Outside firm admits to error, makes corrections. New employee is happy to contribute. Boss is relieved? Thankful? Proud? Embarrassed? Frustrated? All of these?

While Andy was proud to find the CPA firm's error, the ramifications of this find were complex and could potentially impact his job and career in several ways. If he were to take the accolades and full credit for finding the error, he could be putting his boss in a precarious position. After all, the boss reviewed the returns and signed off without finding the tax credit error. While the CPA firm admitted to their error and made the corrections, it was Andy's boss who held the relationship with the CPA firm and thereby was accountable for their hiring and continued services. In essence Andy could embarrass his boss and undercut his boss's authority in one fell swoop.

But that's not what good teammates do. That's not what caring leaders do.

Andy determined the best way to go about the matter was to position the discovery of the error and its subsequent remedy as being a joint effort between him and his boss. Andy's boss was not incompetent; in fact, he was highly competent and well respected. He had simply made a mistake. He was big enough to admit it and wanted Andy to take the credit for finding the error, but Andy wouldn't have any of it. He realized that by having his boss's back in this situation, he would be given the same courtesy in any future scenario. Andy shared the achievement and the associated accolades to build a strong bond between him and his boss but also to show others in the company that the team came first. He shared in success and achievement. He was there when his boss needed him and placed the best interests of the team ahead of his own personal gain.

He embodied the true definition of an exemplary teammate via his selfless action and complete understanding of the significance of building relationships. He put the long-term relationship with his boss ahead of the temptation to take the short-term reward.

> *He cared more about helping his team succeed than about his individual success and placed the relationship with his boss at the forefront of being a great teammate.*

My favorite baseball manager-leader is Tony LaRussa, who offers this premise: "Relationships and building solid ones are the foundation of any great team."

As evidenced in Andy's story, building solid relationships is not only the mark of a great teammate but is also a foundation of exemplary leadership in building a great team. Andy's actions in his story are congruent with Tony LaRussa's premise. And thereby great teammates and great leaders share in the quest to build relationships to ultimately have a positive impact on the team.

Put yourself in Andy's boss's shoes. How would you feel if Andy had gone over your head to others in the organization with the tax credit error? What do you think that action would have done to your perception of Andy and to your newly formed relationship? Aren't you glad he covered for you and shared in the achievement? Aren't you glad you hired Andy to bring his knowledge and commitment to the team and to your company? Don't you wish you had more great teammates like Andy?

Andy said, "It's equally important to make sure your team looks good if you want them to value you as a team member." Andy's actions support that statement wholeheartedly.

Andy Titen, the story you shared with me occurred long before we met and worked together, yet when we did work together, I witnessed your desire to be a great teammate on a daily basis. I am proud to have shared in that experience.

You are an exemplary teammate, leader, and above all, a good person.

Desire: Conscious impulse toward something that promises enjoyment or satisfaction in its attainment.

Leadership in Action: There is nothing as satisfying for a leader as having earned the admiration of his peers for a job well done. By the same token, the desire to achieve admiration can at times overwhelm the desire of getting the job done correctly and can damage existing relationships.

Seeking admiration for one's own benefit may be called self-centeredness and is definitely not something to desire.

LESSON #15: LEADERSHIP AND COACHING WITH COMMITMENT

*To build a strong team, you must see someone
else's strength as a complement to your weakness
and not a threat to your authority.*
—Christine Caine

If you will bear with me, I have one more sports analogy for the lesson learned on coaching. My main point in this lesson learned is a focus on leaders who act and coach others with a long-term benefit in mind and do so as a complement to coaching focused on a short-term, fix-it-now, in-the-moment mindset. There is a time and place for short-term coaching, yet truly impactful, effective coaching lasts much longer than simply immediately addressing a problem at hand. Fix it now and keep it forever go hand in hand in this regard. I promise to get to this principle after a relatable lead-in.

Pat Summit was the head coach of the University of Tennessee (UT) Lady Vols basketball team from 1974 to 2012.

Over the course of her 38 years at the helm of women's basketball at UT, she amassed a .841 overall coaching record, with 1,098 wins against 208 losses. The 1,098 wins were the most in women's college basketball history at the time of her retirement in 2012, only to be surpassed in 2020 by Stanford's head coach Tara VanDerveer and by the University of Connecticut's Geno Auriemma in 2021.

Coach Summit's numerous accomplishments throughout her career included 8 National Collegiate Athletic Association (NCAA) championships, 18 NCAA Regional Final Fours, 16 Southeast Conference (SEC) tournament championships, and 16 SEC regular season championships. These titles earned her the Naismith Coach of the Year Award on 5 separate occasions, induction into the Basketball Hall of Fame in 2000, the John R. Wooden Legends of Coaching Award in 2008, and the *Sports Illustrated* Sportswoman of the Year Award in 2011.

Based on those statistics and the subsequent awards, it is safe to say Coach Summit was an extraordinarily successful basketball coach as far as achieving results through winning, delivering titles, and earning the associated recognition. Coach Summit was known for her disciplined, stern, coach-with-a-purpose approach aimed at immediate results. She was all business all the time and became famous for the "Summit Stare," a look she would impose with the utmost intensity upon a player who was not performing up to expectations. One look in this regard from Coach Summit was all the player needed to know she had better get her act together, fast.

But there is more to the story than what her accolades on the basketball court indicate, as evidenced by her distinguished career accomplishments and awards off the court. Of note are three books she authored or cowrote with Sally Jenkins, which covered subject matter related to her life as a basketball coach, her philosophy on motivation, and subsequently her own battle with Alzheimer's disease. She created the Pat Summit Foundation to build awareness and initiate research for Alzheimer's disease. And of significant note, Coach Summit earned the Presidential Medal of Freedom in 2012, an award given to a United States citizen who demonstrates "an especially meritorious contribution to the security or national interests of the United States, world peace, cultural or other significant public or private endeavors."**

> *Most memorable, however, in terms of her role as a leader in action, is the positive impact, influence, and lasting effect that Coach Summit had on the plethora of collegiate student athletes she worked with through the decades, who embraced her as a role model, mentor, confidant, friend, teacher, and coach.*

One of the more prominent student athletes coached by Pat Summit is the phenomenally talented professional basketball

---

** Executive Order 9586, signed July 6, 1945; Federal Register 10 FR 8523, July 10, 1945.

player turned sports commentator Candace Parker. I can say I have a connection to this high-profile person as my stepdaughter Carin, and my two sons Chris and Corey attended Naperville Central High School (NCHS) in Naperville, Illinois, the same high school as Candace Parker. OK, so that connection to Candace Parker may be a stretch, but I am proud to say I was able to follow her high school, college, and the pro career and always felt a connection to her.

She was the high school phenom I would read about in the local *Naperville Sun* newspaper and was the first female in the state of Illinois as a fifteen-year-old sophomore to slam dunk a basketball. Candace was, and still is, the only two-time USA Today High School Player of the Year award winner, having led NCHS to back-to-back state titles in 2003 and 2004 and having graduated from the school as its all-time leader in points scored with 2,768. She was a Gatorade Female Athlete of the Year and a USA World Junior Gold Medal Champion in 2004.

Candace was the local kid who made good and went on to play for Coach Summit at UT and was the first woman to slam dunk a basketball in an NCAA tournament game. She led Coach Summit's 2007 and 2008 teams to NCAA championships and topped that off by being an Olympic Gold Medalist at the 2008 Beijing games and then repeated the same gold medal performance at the 2012 games in London. Candace was a University Division 1 Academic All-American and graduated with her incoming class in 2008.

During the course of her twelve-year professional career, Candace was the Women's National Basketball Association (WNBA) Rookie of the Year, six-time All-WNBA First Team Star, 5-time WNBA All-Star, two-time WNBA Most Valuable Player (MVP), 2016 WNBA Finals MVP, and a 2016 WNBA Champion with the Los Angeles Sparks.

Most memorable, however, among the outcomes of Coach Summit's legacy and her influence on Candace Parker as a person was Candace's post-WNBA 2016 championship game interview wherein she humbly and emotionally said, "This is for Pat."

With all the praise, publicity, media scrutiny and notoriety that comes with being a professional athlete, it would seem obvious that people at that level of public attention may get wound up in themselves and their own agenda. They may let their egos get in the way of their purpose. They may let their egos get in the way of their teammates, coaches, and maybe even their own families.

But not Candace Parker, at that moment when she could have easily been caught up in celebrating her team's championship. In just a few simple words, she articulated the most important compliment a coach could ask of her players. Coach Summit's impact on Candace was more than short term; it was lifelong.

Candace's ultimate success wasn't just about her achievement in the moment; it was about paying homage to a person that helped her get to where she wanted to go to as an athlete and as a person. She didn't let the glamour of the moment distract her from remembering Coach Summit, her college coach removed by eight years, who had passed away from Alzheimer's disease just a few months earlier in 2016. I believe her statement is a direct result of Coach Summit's significant positive coaching influence. I believe Candace Parker embraced Coach Summit's disciplined coaching style for not only the short-term benefit of becoming a better basketball player but also the opportunity to become an overall better person in the long term.

> *There is an ongoing debate about whether a great player can make a coach great at their job or if it is a great coach that brings out the best in a player to make that player great. Maybe the answer lies in the fact that both coach and player need each other to be great and together achieve great things.*

What I believe to be true, however, in this regard is the concept of the player being "coachable." The student must have an open mindset, recognize the advanced knowledge of the coach, and be willing to accept the coach's directive to improve their own performance. In the same light, the coach must be open to accepting a player's input and recognizing a player's strengths and opportunities and be willing to put aside judgment during the course of implementing process and personal improvement. In short, coach and player are both empowered to think for each other's benefit and are committed to each other to achieve a common goal. I believe this principle to be the foundation of effective leadership coaching. It's not just about coaching to the task for results; it's about coaching to the person for personal development.

It is similar in a business setting. Managers are trained to coach in the short term. The employee presents a situation that requires managerial input to fix a problem. The manager does what she does best and provides a solution. Problem solved, situation fixed, move on to the next scenario. This type of coaching supports a command-and-control environment. It is easy to spot and easy to implement. Employee asks a question; manager provides an answer. This is the ultimate short-term approach with no focus on employee development or long-term thinking. It is reactionary, task-oriented management.

Leadership coaching focuses on a much more developmental approach that includes a teachable moment where the leader offers support and guidance. Coaching in itself is not a onetime event. In general terms coaching an employee or coworker is continuous and ongoing as a foundation of development for both the coach and the person being coached. Coaching in this manner assumes a "teach to help them grow" model with much more emphasis being placed on guiding the person being coached to figure out problems on their own.

In the simple situation suggested in the previous paragraphs, a coworker comes to the leader with a problem. Rather than the leader telling the coworker how to solve the problem, the leader asks more questions and listens to fully comprehend the situation with the intent of allowing the solution-seeker to figure out the answer on her own. It is an ask-and-listen scenario versus a tell-and-sell solution. It provides an opportunity to teach and develop. I believe leaders should coach in this manner, with the intent of facilitating a coworker's long-term development in the majority of situations rather than telling them what to do in the short term.

Ultimately the coach and player, or the leader and coworker, thrive best in a learning organization, one that places emphasis on continuous improvement both personally and professionally via an open and collaborative environment. Leaders of these organizations strive to remove the barriers and limitations associated with short-term managerial fixes and replace that environment with a culture that prospers via mutual respect and collaborative learning. They are experts in communicating this message and model the message throughout their daily routine.

The best leader-coach in this type of culture emphasizes support throughout the development process and hesitates to judge at any point along the way. There are no preconceived judgments, prejudices, or assumptions that may blind the leader-coach from fully understanding both the long-term effect on the person in need of attention and the short-term solution to the problem that needs to be addressed. The leader-coach becomes a facilitator of collaborative problem-solving that benefits all participants.

We can break down leadership coaching in action into four separate and basic categories to further address the relationship between leader-coach and coworker. There are of course more complex scenarios that may not fall into one of these four distinct categories, and there are scenarios that blend or cross over between the four categories, but for simplicity of point, these general categories provide a solid foundation of leader-coach responsibilities.

- **Direct**—this occurs, as described previously, when the recipient is task-oriented, the coach is solution-oriented, and there is little collaborative or developmental emphasis. The entire process is focused on ask a question, get an answer. From a coach's perspective, it is centered on "I see your problem, and I will tell you what to do to fix it." This category also applies to those individuals who are learning a task for the first time. They don't know how to do the job, so they must be trained rather than coached in this regard.

- **Collaborative**—this is the scenario whereby the coach-leader uses a more guided approach with the co-worker by asking questions, listening with purpose, and feeding back potential options to address the problem. The intent of the coaching conversation is to get the co-worker to think, to draw them out, to help them answer the question at hand on their own. Many times the co-worker is just looking for a verification of the decision they want to make; they need affirmation and support. Allowing them to come to their own conclusion and providing an agreement is more about their gaining confidence in their thinking than anything else. I believe it is imperative for the coach to instill, build, and enhance a coworker's confidence in any and all scenarios. Getting a coworker to think on their own and solve their own challenges contributes to their individual development.

- **Situational**—this is the widely accepted coaching model whereby the coach identifies the skill set (competence) and readiness level (commitment) of the individual and responds with coaching suitable to the individual's categorization. Coaching can vary from needs-of-the-moment telling and selling to more elaborate observation and speculation, depending on the complexity of the scenario and the people involved. I support situational coaching as a well-regarded methodology for two reasons: first, it reminds the coach to treat each person and each scenario individually as a unique opportunity even when there are similarities among people and occurrences of similar circumstances, and second, because a coach develops experience and personal growth along the way. The fact that situational coaching works is good reason for a leader-coach to become proficient in this methodology.

- **On their own**—this is really more applicable to the non-coach situation. The coworker is empowered to do their job, solve their challenges, take initiative, and assist others if needed with little to no supervision. This is accepted simply because the coworker is fully capable of handling their work challenges in an appropriate manner and has the desire to do so without need of direction. It is best to leave them alone, stay out of their way, and let them do their jobs.

Here is a formula of a simple yet effective leader-coach method for problem-solving or for personal development that I found exceptionally helpful throughout my career. It is one that can be adapted to almost any situation that requires an individual—or a team of people, for that matter—to act with purpose to solve an issue or change a behavior.

- **Establish a goal** ---What is it that we are trying to accomplish? Define the end result, the outcome, the success we want to achieve. Write it out in a clear and concise manner so there is no doubt in the minds of any of the participants.
- **Identify the reasons**---What is negatively impacting our goal achievement? What do we know, what do we need to know, what are the barriers preventing us from achieving our goal? What's stopping us from success? What's holding us back from the desired improvement?
- **Look for options**---What are the alternatives, what are our choices, and what can we do to solve the problem,

to challenge the negative reason? What solutions can we present? This brainstorming can be guided, or it can be left to the individual or team to address, but it has to be in depth. The options provided must be detailed to allow for all participants to see the solution as reality, that the goal can be achieved.

- **Act**---Most importantly, answer the question, What are you going to personally do to achieve your goal? Follow up that question with one or more of these: How *committed* are you to achieving your goal? How likely are you going to be to put forth the effort required to achieve your goal? How motivated are you in this regard? On a scale of 1 to 10, how will you hold yourself accountable to achieving the goal?

The final bullet point listed above is the differentiator between coaching in a short-term, task-oriented manner and coaching for the long-term and influencing people to personally develop. The impact is based on commitment to learn, grow, develop, change, and improve while accepting the coaching for the long haul. The formula provides an outline for the leader-coach to follow, yet nothing in regard to actually seeing a positive outcome to the situation will be accomplished without the firm commitment of the individual or team to follow through and act on the selected option.

Commitment from both coach-leader and coworker, employee, teammate, or player is required to ensure the proposed solution is enacted. It has to be put into play and executed accordingly for the solution to be successful. More importantly, it has to be accepted by both coach and player as a positive influence on the desired outcome in the short term and agreed upon as a behavioral change for the long term.

Coaching with commitment as a leader allows the person being influenced to be empowered, develop new insight, think creatively, enhance their performance, and improve their communication skill set. But it also provides that individual with an opportunity to learn for the long haul. It provides the individual the opportunity to develop outside of the job performance or the workplace interaction. Coaching with commitment influences an individual to develop great habits and to develop as a caring, thoughtful person.

Much the same as Candace Parker paid tribute to her college coach and mentor Pat Summit. Her words were short, her statement brief, yet "This is for Pat" carried much importance. This statement spoke to the commitment of player to coach, the mutual respect gained, the positive influence created, and the impact a coach can have on a person's development. That's a perfect example of coaching to a desired outcome. An outcome built on modeling what you coach and being committed to your model.

Communicate: To convey knowledge of or information about; make known; to transmit information, thought, or feeling so that it is satisfactorily received or understood.

Leadership in Action: Great leader-coaches know the positive feeling that goes along with conveying knowledge to a fellow employee that allows that employee the opportunity to learn, develop their skill set, and improve their job performance. Yet the secret to success is in knowing how to communicate the message so the recipient gets it and will subsequently commit and act on the message.

My wife is particularly good at conducting these coaching conversations with me as the recipient. Mainly because I know my next meal is riding on whether or not I get it, commit, and take the correct action.

LESSON #16: COMMUNICATE WITH PURPOSE

Courage is what it takes to stand up and speak;
courage is also what it takes to sit down and listen.
—Sir Winston Churchill

Westminster College is a renowned private liberal arts college established in 1851 in Fulton, Missouri, a rural area in the upper middle of the state in America's heartland. Sprawling over a pleasant and cozy eighty-six acres, Westminster College is the home at last count to 750 undergraduate students, the majority of whom come to the college from their home state of Missouri. It provides a safe, diverse, and healthy environment and appeals to students who prefer a smaller college campus and the opportunity to be recognized as an individual rather than as a statistic, the latter of which students experience at larger, more populous institutions of higher education.

Students also choose Westminster College for the high-quality academics, personal learning environment, comradery with fellow students, and a choice of twenty-nine majors and thir-ty-nine minors that provide a foundation for future learning and career success. Of significant importance are the outcomes associated with graduating from Westminster College. Graduates enjoy a 98 percent placement rating in pursuing a job or in attending graduate school and consistently rank in the top 15 percent in national graduate earnings.

Destroyed by a fire in 1909 that left only the Greek-style columns remaining on campus, Westminster College was rebuilt gradually over the years to become what it is today, the centerpiece of liberal arts colleges in the Midwest. In 1969 the church of Saint Mary the Virgin Aldermanbury was moved from England to the Westminster campus and is a primary contributor to campus's ambiance. The church adds to the visual elegance of the campus but speaks more to the historical significance it represents as a bond between the old and the new, England/Europe and the United States. In this regard the college has become a stopping point for leaders in all fields as evidenced by the list of important people who have visited Westminster College to recognize that bond.

Via a series of lectures throughout the years, Westminster College has provided the stage for numerous well-recognized and relevant global political dignitaries, including presidents Harry Truman, Gerald Ford, Ronald Reagan, and George H. W. Bush. International figures Mikhail Gorbachev and Margaret Thatcher also graced the Westminster College stage and provided thought-provoking, challenging, and informative speeches in tune with world events—contradictory to static viewpoints and intriguing to still developing college-aged minds.

Yet while all of these renowned individuals provided a lasting impression on the Westminster attendees, none is more heralded for his contribution than Sir Winston Churchill, who delivered his famous "Sinews of Peace" speech at Westminster in 1946, after the end of World War II. It is commonly referred to as "The Iron Curtain Speech," and here Churchill provided his thoughts on the postwar era and in essence foretold of the coming Cold War. Churchill articulated not only his wisdom and knowledge of world events and the impact the aftermath of the war would have on the immediate future, but he also correctly predicted the fallout between East and West and in particular the faltering, dividing, and deteriorating relationship between the Allies and the Soviets. His speech in this regard was the epitome of preparation, confidence, and speaking ability.

Churchill was the living definition of a leader communicating with purpose.

Churchill exemplified a leader in action throughout his term as the prime minister of England in perhaps the most difficult set of circumstances one could possibly imagine. In 1940 England was the last remaining blockade to the Axis powers' potential European domination. The island and its inhabitants were subjected to daily bombardment from Nazi Germany air raids and the inevitable death and destruction that is part of war's hell. Lesser leaders may have succumbed to the intolerable conditions and pressure to seek peace through submission, but Churchill would not do this. He would not give in; he would not surrender his country and its people to the tyranny. He would not relinquish his spirit nor give up the fight. Instead, he would use his superior communications skills and leadership ability to invigorate, inspire, rally, and build a supportive base designed to withstand the Nazi aggressor while he formulated a strategic plan to defeat this worst of all enemies.

Churchill let his actions define his leadership skills as he regularly and consistently communicated with England's people. Instead of going into hiding as some weaker counterparts did at the time, Churchill became more visible to the populous. He regularly broadcasted inspiring radio messages, consistently reminding his fellow countrymen that he would not give up or give in and that they in turn should remain confident, hopeful, encouraged, and determined.

During his speech to Parliament in 1940, Churchill warned of the possible invasion by Nazi Germany yet held firm to his commitment to remain steadfast. He maintained his focus on victory in the upcoming battles, in winning the war, in repelling the aggressor, and in returning to a peaceful society free from tyranny.

In building his support to fight for freedom, Churchill passionately reminded Parliament of his vision and delivered an inspiring message designed to leave no doubt about his intents. When desperation seemed more a common outlet, Churchill instilled motivation. There was no bend in his delivery, no sway in his determination, no hesitation in telling Parliament his ultimate endgame: "You ask, what is our aim? I can answer with one word: it is victory, victory at all costs, victory in spite of terror, victory, however long and hard the road may be; for without victory, there is no survival. Let that be realized; no survival for the British Empire, no survival for all that the British Empire has stood for...and I say, come then let us go forward with our united strength."

He reiterated his vision of victory and to "fight on the seas and oceans, we shall fight with growing confidence and growing strength in the air, we shall defend our island, whatever the cost may be. We shall fight on the beaches, we shall fight on the landing grounds, we shall fight in the fields and in the streets, we shall fight in the hills; we shall never surrender."

Churchill realized the importance of being seen as a leader in touch with his constituency, cognizant of their situation, and regularly visited his civilian counterparts and British soldiers at airfields, naval bases, and along the front lines in North Africa and Europe. He engaged in action to complement his inspiring rhetoric and showed his leadership by backing up his words via his presence. And the rest of the world took note.

Via his actions, his leadership skill set, and his ability as a prolific orator, Churchill became larger-than-life at a time when people needed a hero to stand up to the tyranny.

Churchill embodied leadership communication principles in his everyday actions, and this set the framework for others upon which to learn and develop. He consistently engaged in the following leadership communications best practices.

- **Vision**—leaders clearly define what the future looks like and provide details on where they want to take their organization. They provide a focal point of expectations and outcomes based on personal and shared goals and aspirations.
- **Values**—the leader defines who we are as an organization, what we believe in, how our culture supports the foundation of our beliefs, and how we act on our beliefs via our culture.
- **Strategy**—the leader presents the strategic plan and vision in layers of importance to ensure the message is understood within the organization, as if speaking directly to people in their functional role. This includes big picture, managerial, operational, functional, and tactical layers.
- **Consistent messaging**—the overarching message remains the same throughout the course of the undertaking, there are no inconsistencies or disconnects, and the

intent is well understood and accepted as fact.

- **Frequent messaging**—the leader provides the communications platform at regular intervals to ensure the communication is received; this also provides an opportunity for the leader to engage often with the organization shareholders and stakeholders alike.

- **Message content**—leaders use the opportunity to inspire, invigorate, and build the organization's confidence. They are enthusiastic yet serious and focused on presenting while staying honest to themselves and to the commitment they make to the organization. They speak with candor and conviction and build their own credibility via their serious approach to difficult situations.

- **Feedback**—leaders are aware of the need to accept feedback and a diversity of thoughts. They are confident in providing this opportunity, and they readily receive input to improve their message and its organizational acceptance. They welcome the chance to be measured and to have their message critiqued.

- **Listen**—exemplary leaders practice the art of effective communications by being extraordinary listeners willing and able to hear all viewpoints. They build on their own ability by listening and engaging with a diversity of thought; they are empathetic and understanding.

- **Influence**—they are strong in their will to compel others to support their direction yet do so with a skill level that is not manipulative, selfish, or fake in nature. They influence in a positive and resourceful manner. They get others involved and gain their support and loyalty.

- **Bond together**—exemplary leaders use the communications platform to bring people and organizations together, they value a common goal and guide others to value like principles. They build rather than divide.

In Churchill's own words: "*Of all the talents bestowed upon men, none is so precious as the gift of orator. Whoever can command this power is still formidable.*"

Housed in the foundation of the church of Saint Mary the Virgin Aldermanbury on the campus of Westminster College is a truly remarkable treasure. America's National Churchill Museum occupies the lower level of the church and serves as a shrine dedicated to the great orator and leader. This hidden secret provides an homage to the greatness of Winston Churchill and offers a detailed perspective on his life in the military, as a politician, as an artist and writer.

A visit to Westminster College and America's National Churchill Museum is well worth the trip to Middle America. You will find the people at the college and the museum, along with the residents of Fulton, Missouri, to be hospitable and down-to-earth. To fully appreciate Churchill and understand his impact on modern society, take the time to see the campus and the museum. It is also very much an opportunity to hear and see

Churchill for the outstanding orator, leader, and communicator that numerous historians have recognized in countless works.

When you visit the museum and absorb the plethora of Churchill history, whether visiting for the first time or as a repeat visitor, I hope you will keep my thoughts in mind and see Churchill in the same light as I do.

It's fitting that the museum is set in the foundation of the church. Metaphorically speaking, it is easy for me to think of Churchill as a steadfast and unwavering rock on which the church was built. A significant leader, statesman, and orator who led his country through its darkest days. Built upon his legend stands a structure of peace, tranquility, and worship that serves as a shining light of hope for all who experience its remarkable beauty.

I didn't make this connection during my time at Westminster College, yet the symbolism is moving and made quite an impression. It also left me with chills.

And it provided a significant lesson learned.

Visionary: Having or marked by foresight and imagination

Leadership in Action: To be a visionary leader, one must have a clear twenty-twenty sense of the past. While history will not repeat itself, similar circumstances will occur. The exemplary leader recognizes the circumstance and acts with knowledge of what to say and do.

It is definitely an advantage to have clear sight on what is coming by knowing what previously happened.

LESSON #17: LEADERSHIP AND COMMUNITY

*Being good is commendable, but only when it
is combined with doing good is it useful.*
—Unknown

Seriously? Another sports analogy for the opening of this lesson learned? Well, yes. But this opening ties in so well with the subject matter that I couldn't help myself. The lesson learned is about a tremendous human being, friend, mentor, and leader who exemplified what giving back to the community means. I know you will enjoy this connection. At least I hope you will.

Payne Stewart was a professional golfer who won eleven United States Professional Golf Association (PGA) events, including three major championships, during his short-lived career. His most celebrated wins were the 1989 PGA Championship and the 1991 and 1999 US Open events. The Springfield, Missouri, native represented the United States on five Ryder Cup teams in competition versus European counterparts in the late 1980s and early 1990s. He was consistently ranked as one of the top ten golfers in the world during the same time frame prior to his untimely death at the age of forty-two in an airplane crash in October of 1999, just four months after his second US Open win.

Important to the golf world and especially to his fan base, Payne Stewart was renowned for his love of golf traditions. He was a popular figure among golf enthusiasts not only because of his ability to strike a golf ball with precision and play the game at such a high level but also because of his oftentimes flamboyant, outrageous, and colorful wardrobe. Stewart was the golfer who wore knickers, the short, knee-length pants matched with knee high stockings, topped off with a lid, more commonly known as a flat golf cap, on his head. Stewart was the golfer who paid tribute to generations of golfers before him who regularly wore the golf knickers uniform. Wearing knickers on the golf course was stylish and fashionable in the early 1900s. This same type of outfit was viewed as dashingly bold and extravagant for Stewart's generation.

At one time Stewart had a contract with the National Football League (NFL) whereby he would wear a knickers ensemble that matched the uniform colors of the NFL team most strongly associated with or in close proximity to the city of the golf tournament in which he was entered. The hometown fans loved it. Cross-marketing in this manner was a hit and enamored Stewart to the local populous. He wore the local team's colors as an homage to their city, and the fans ate it up.

The PGA presents the Payne Stewart Award each year to a player who shows respect for the traditions of the game, commitment to uphold the game's heritage of charitable support, and professional and meticulous presentation of himself and the sport through his dress and conduct.

If the average weekend golfer wants to wear knickers to play golf, it is recommended that such person also have the required skill set to back up the outfit via a high-compete level of play or be willing to submit to constant ridicule from fellow golfers. Wearing knickers is a bold statement, one which some would interpret as a mark of confidence. Certainly wearing knickers at the local golf course for a round of play provides an opportunity for other golfers to point, stare, laugh, ask a question like "Who ya' caddying for today?" and leaves them wondering if it's Halloween or if the circus is in town. Others would view this ensemble as outdated or think the wearer was trying to gain attention. From my own experience, they would be correct on both accounts.

I've never considered myself a good golfer and certainly not one who would call attention to myself by wearing a loudly colored knickers ensemble. I am confident enough in my golf game to wear items that match and allow me to blend in with the scenery. I do not wish to call any attention to my golf ability—or lack thereof. Most definitely I would never wear knickers. Until I did. And I did so at the behest of a former mentor, leader, and friend, John Holbrook.

I had the pleasure of working with John during my DeVry days and came to know him as a kind, generous, humble human being who taught me quite a bit about leadership from a humanistic, caring standpoint. Noted for his "top of the day" greeting, "How's your plan?" work camaraderie, and his "power of one" mantra, John was one of the most likable individuals I had the opportunity to work with. He always presented himself to me with a smile on his face and was more concerned about how I was doing than with his agenda. I couldn't help but want to work for John simply based on how he treated me as a person. John presented himself as a happy human regardless of the challenges and personal issues he faced.

> *To this day John is the only leader for whom I worked who actually demonstrated his fondness of people and his true belief in the importance of respecting people by not only knowing their name but also by knowing how to pronounce their name* correctly *without hesitation.*

He did this to my amazement at a national managers meeting where we were gathered for the first time as a team under John's leadership. While this was his second stint with DeVry, he had only been back as the vice president of enrollment for a short amount of time, approximately four months. In that time he managed to visit as many DeVry campuses and meet as many of the staff as possible, and at this admissions leadership gathering, he was meeting several of his campus directors of admissions for the first time. There were approximately ninety of us present at the meeting, including home office staff, trainers, and admissions leaders. On the final day of the three-day event, John stood in front of the group and at a point in his presentation where he was reminding us of the importance of our commitment to our students, he confidently went around the room and recognized by first and last name everyone who was in the room. He had met some of these people only a couple of days before and in what might have been a challenge for another person new to an organization, John without hesitation pointed at each one of us in the room and pronounced our first and last names perfectly! He was even able to muster Ka-lau-wee-ack exactly as it should be said when he came to me. This display of acknowledgment wasn't a cheap parlor trick or a magician's illusion.

> *John's ability to learn and acknowledge our names was a true demonstration of leadership in action. He proved a point that he actually cared enough about us to learn who we were and how to correctly pronounce our names.*

If you've ever worked for someone who couldn't correctly pronounce your name or worked with someone who couldn't correctly pronounce the name of someone on your team, you know exactly what I'm talking about.

John's remarkably friendly personality and loose management style made him an easy person with which to work. Yet John was serious and focused when speaking of the "power of one." His mantra translates to the effort a person makes to attain a goal, achieve a desired result, or help someone else in need. Whether it is making one more phone call or getting one more coworker engaged in their work or by doing one extra thing to guide someone to achieve their goal, the "power of one" is a consistent reminder of how going the extra mile or working a little harder and keeping a commitment can work for the benefit of all involved. John would often remind me and those of us in his managerial reporting line that achieving big accomplishments sometimes came down to just doing one more thing the right way.

He accepted this mantra as a foundation for how he viewed his position as a leader in a major organization and how a leader should go about his business in building relationships within the organization. But he also viewed this mantra as concrete when it came to a leader's commitment to giving back to the community.

So it was no surprise to me that once John found out I enjoyed playing a round of golf, he asked me to join him at one of the local courses to get away from work for a little while. It was a surprise to me, however, when John showed up wearing the brightest, loudest, ocean blue knickers, complete with matching flat hat. I thought to myself, *Either he's really good at this golf game or he's just out to embarrass both himself and me.*

As it turned out, it was more of the latter, but it was all in good fun. John didn't take his golf game too seriously, and he wanted to enjoy the opportunity to spend time on the links and pay respect to the traditionalists, the golf-knickers-wearing participants from years gone by. But he also wanted to pay respect to Payne Stewart and the foundation that he and his friends supported throughout the year.

John Holbrook, along with his friend Bill Holtry, was the founder of the Knicker National Argyle Champions Tour (The Knick-Nac Tour), a group of golfers who wore knickers and played in various events during the summer months of golf season. Early in its beginnings, the Knick-Nac Tour golfers would play in a variety of events to raise funds for the Payne Stewart Family Foundation, which has as its mission "to primarily assist with programs that allow children and youth to have new opportunities to experience the joy of Christianity."***

As the Knick-Nac Tour membership grew and chapters began to spring up in various cities across the United States, the charitable causes took on new meanings. The local chapter presidents looked for charities that were start-ups, those without a lot of national support, or those that had national support but were focused on helping a local individual through tough times or those that had a particular local interest to the community. The entire concept of the Knick-Nac Tour took on a new meaning as an opportunity for any level of golfer to participate in a local golf

---

***   https://paynestewartfamilyfoundation.com.

outing, have fun, play golf, and make a charitable donation to a great cause.

It was inevitable that John would "draft" me to join the local Chicago chapter of the Knick-Nac Tour, and along with my coworkers Mark Buck and Rick Borowiak, we became "The Chicago Four." Outfitted with knickers, argyles, and lids, we played in several golf outings for charity throughout the years, most notably for Juvenile Diabetes and the American Cancer Society, with proceeds going to a local member of those organizations in need. As our opportunities to play in events increased, so did the number of our knickers outfits. After all, we couldn't be seen wearing the same knickers over and over, so the wardrobe of colorful combinations grew in our closets. Although I myself was partial to a relatively safe but bold combination of red, black, and white.

When Mark took over the leadership of the Chicago Knick-Nac Tour chapter, he expanded the membership, the charities, and the contributions. Successful outings were held, with over one hundred golfers willing to contribute their support to local charitable organizations such as the Kylie Arnold Cancer Fund, and Camp Out from Cancer. We even participated in an event to help support one of the local high school hockey teams that was not eligible for state funding as the sport is not recognized by the Illinois High School Association.

Sponsoring and playing in these outings was an opportunity to give back to the community. It wasn't just about playing golf;

it was about playing golf for a better purpose. It was about enjoying a round of golf and making a charitable contribution in support of a better cause. It was about the feeling a person gets when doing something for others. It was about having a sense of pride in knowing that the efforts made were going to help others regardless of their situation.

> *Leaders act and live up to the premise of doing well by doing good. What they do via their actions in support of others is a significant example of responsibility to community and a true characteristic of leadership in action.*

Numerous organizations and major corporations provide an opportunity for their employees to give back to the community via sponsorships, donations of money and time, and partnerships in walk-a-thons and large-scale events. I had the pleasure of participating and supporting many such events throughout my career in leadership positions. While all provided a worthwhile, rewarding experience and a great sense of contribution back to the community, the opportunity to play golf in the Knick-Nac Tour was unique.

I have John Holbrook to thank for this experience. To many of his coworkers, John was a mentor, coach, confidant, and friend. He was the godfather who would listen to any and all problems and concerns with no preconceived prejudice or disinterest. He genuinely wanted to understand and help others as much as he possibly could.

I also have John to thank for the unique experience of wearing golf knickers. No one told me ahead of time that the elastic band at the bottom of each pant leg would leave such an impressionable mark on my upper calf. Kind of like a rope burn. Kind of like having the circulation cut off in your legs. I do not understand how the golfers of years ago were able to wear these things day in and day out on the golf course. Wearing knickers for a four-and-a-half-hour round of golf was plenty as far as I was concerned. But while perhaps not as comfortable as I would have liked, I always reminded myself that wearing knickers was more about a mindset than a fashion statement. It was about my willingness to look the part while contributing to a worthy cause.

John Holbrook provided a perfect leadership in action example via his love for golf but also via his love for people. He was leadership in action when it came to providing an example of what leaders should do from a sense of community. Unfortunately, John lost his valiant eighteen-month battle against cancer and passed away at the way too early age of sixty-one, in 2012. It seems like only yesterday when I could hear him saying, "Top of the morning." But his legacy of leadership and giving back to the community lives on. The next Knick-Nac outing will definitely be in his memory.

Confidence: A feeling or consciousness of one's powers or of reliance on one's circumstances; faith or belief that one will act in a right, proper, or effective way.

Leadership in Action: A well-respected leader once told me that being confident can be compared to drinking scotch. Not only do you have to acquire a taste for it, but others will know when you've had a little too much of it as well. Be sure you don't get wrapped up in having a little too much confidence, others may interpret that as arrogance.

Moderation is key.

LESSON #18: LEADERSHIP AND CAPACITY

*In my own deepening understanding of myself, I find
my capacity to serve others is deepened as well.*
—Mary Anne Radmacher

We all know people who stretch themselves too thin by misman-
aging their time, energy, and priorities. Their perception is mis-
informed, their efforts are misdirected, and their results are mis-
aligned to expectations. They constantly juggle projects, plans,
and platforms and most times are guilty of dropping the ball on
desired outcomes. They are more likely to engage in every possible social event offered in their organization because they love
to participate. But their over-participation in the social aspect at
work causes their productivity to suffer.

In the end socializing becomes their work.

Because they regularly mismanage their participation and
subsequent activities, they end up challenged to handle their

work, balance their life, follow through on priorities, or maintain a healthy relationship.

In short, they overcommit.

They do not understand or acknowledge their own capacity. They have difficulty saying no. They say yes far too often because they don't have a solid handle on their capacity to perform to desired expectations. They take on too much too often. Failing to understand their capacity hurts their productivity, their coworker's productivity, damages their relationships, and wreaks havoc on their ability to complete assignments.

Alternately, we all know people who are perfectly willing and able to take on "stretch assignments." These people seem to have a knack for being able to handle their work, balance their lives, make the most of their time, and still have opportunity to challenge themselves. They are the people in an organization recognized for their potential to develop their skill set, to grow by taking on more responsibility or a special assignment, and they are perfectly capable of delivering on expected results.

They manage themselves and balance through the challenge.

And while it may not be easy to complete—hence the "stretch assignment" moniker—they are able to deliver. They are easily identified as the high performers, high-potential people in the organization. They may not fully understand their capacity, but they are great at prioritization and are able to focus their efforts in the areas that provide maximum productivity.

They readily accept the opportunity to expand their capacity.

Increased capacity in the sense of being able to take on additional assignments or a heavier workload is in direct proportion to a person improving their individual skill set and becoming more proficient at their job. With knowledge, experience, and proficiency, the opportunity presents itself to increase capacity.

However, being able to take on a greater workload is only one aspect of capacity. In the true sense of the term, ability is defined as gaining knowledge or developing a skill set, while capacity is defined as the potential to develop a skill set (i.e., does the proficient manager possess the capacity to develop into an esteemed leader?).

Thus leaders understand their own capacity in several different areas outside of their ability to accept additional assignments or workloads. Effective leaders grasp the concept of capacity in three distinct yet related areas.

- **People**—effective leaders are self-aware, they know who they are, they know their strengths and opportunities, and how they are perceived in the organization. They also have the capacity to understand and be aware of others in terms of this same appreciation of who they are, strengths and opportunities, and perception. Critical to the relationship between the leader being self-aware and their understanding of their relationship with others is the leader's grasp of how those elements are situationally interpreted. Effective leaders recognize the situation. They also recognize that the situation may change, the variables may evolve. Effective leaders recognize the situational change required and are able to pivot quickly in their strategy, direction, process, and desire for continuous personal and organizational improvement.

- **Ability**—effective leaders have a firm grasp of their own experience, knowledge, and skill set. They understand their particular talents and proficiencies and leverage those talents in their approach to their interactions and to their work. They worked hard during the course of their leadership journey to expand their interpersonal skills, knowledge, and proficiency to place themselves in a position to grow and take on greater, more challenging assignments. Their confidence is in tune with their competence, and vice versa.

- **Commitment**—effective leaders exemplify the commitment, dedication to purpose, and intensity of effort required to successfully accomplish their undertakings. In other words, they go at it with a full-focus, all-in, personal passion. They are relentless in their dedication to purpose. Their peers and coworkers have an expectation in this regard, and the effective leader is fully aware of the backlash or ramifications if the level of commitment is lower than anticipated by the constituents. Yet effective leaders are skilled at balancing their commitment intensity level and the relationship/interaction level within the organization. They are passionate about purpose yet are appreciative of others so as not to achieve their success and force their commitment to deliver results at the expense of others.

Effective leaders display a capacity to use and understand complex information. They have the aptitude to comprehend information, analyze the information, break it down, and determine how best to apply it for the benefit of their organization. This skill set is critical in the decision-making process and in communicating the decision to the organization. They understand the complexities and are able to deliver the message in a way that eliminates the possibility of confusion by the receivers. Effective leaders use a variety of methodologies to deliver the message, yet critical to their effectiveness is being able to present the message in terms that are easily relatable and understandable to the audience.

Effective leaders display the capacity to influence others. Critical to leadership is the ability to direct others without being direct in nature. Of note are the leaders who can influence others to solve their own problems, issues, and challenges by creating an environment of empowered thinking. Allowing others to have a voice is part of a collaborative environment, yet effective leaders fully understand how to guide others to act with confidence in addressing problems and in finding solutions to those problems.

Effective leaders understand the concept of leading based on demand. They recognize the situation and are willing and able to provide the required leadership others are counting on in times of crisis. Remember that Joshua Lawrence Chamberlain was thrust into a leadership role and was required to assess a critical situation in a matter of a few moments; the nature of the situation placed a massive demand on his leadership skills. He could have withdrawn yet chose to be decisive and aggressive in the course of battle. I imagine the demand and the serious nature of the situation forced him to be less than calm, cool, and collective in his decision-making process. In fact, I imagine it was quite harrowing, stressful, and intensely aggravated. Yet he made the right decision. He acted. He met the demand. If he flinched, he didn't show it. He acted.

Effective leaders are the first to remain calm, cool, and collective. They present their professional presence to ensure others are encouraged in the same regard. Regardless of severity of crisis, the effective leader displays the capacity to remain level-headed, knowing that others will respond and react based on the leader's response and reaction. Panic is not the answer in a crisis.

Remaining calm in the storm demonstrates sound foundational leadership and provides the peace of mind required to weather the storm.

Effective leaders also understand and take ownership of the capacity to lead based on demand. My friend Laurie Bianchi says it best in these simple but profound words: "Know the value of your people." This statement applies to numerous interactions and scenarios, including your people's productivity and impact on the organization's bottom line, their influence and association with coworkers and customers, their ability to problem solve, be critical thinkers, demonstrate empathy, and live and perform to the expectations of the core values.

It also applies to their market worth (i.e., their buying power should they determine to take their talents to another organization). Leaders should be keenly aware of the value of those in their stead from a personal as well as professional standpoint. What would it cost the organization in terms of time, effort, productivity, downtime, resources, and morale should a key member of the team leave for another opportunity? The effective leader is cognizant of people power and always aware of the possibility of replacement costs and impact on the organization.

It also applies to a critical aspect in measuring a leader's overall success when it comes to either taking on the work individually or in delegating the work to a coworker. Note I didn't use the term "subordinate." Effective leaders recognize the value of their coworkers and their ability to support the leader's platform, execute the strategy associated with the platform, and follow through to successful fruition. Effective leaders at times may challenge coworkers to stretch their own capacity in an effort to guide them to develop, become more proficient, and add to their skill set, yet they will rarely delegate an overly complex assignment to a person who does not demonstrate the ability and willingness to bring the assignment to proper fruition.

Exemplary leaders know the value of their coworkers' capacity and delegate assignments designed to build confidence, competency, knowledge, and experience during the course of bringing the assignment to its fruition.

Effective leaders also demonstrate their capacity to use information to make intelligent and better-informed decisions. They are in tune with their organization at all levels. They take the time to engage coworkers regardless of their position in the organization and to stay close to the core foundation of the business. They are well informed, open to suggestion, willing to listen, actively engaged in finding out what is going on to help them make better decisions for the organization and do so with no preconceived opinion about what they think the process or the platform should be. They are open-minded and approachable. They seek information and absorb the detail with an eager attitude.

If this is not the most important part of capacity, it is certainly somewhere near the top: *Effective leaders know their success in leading others is a direct result of their capacity to serve others.*

In fact, servant leadership is founded on this principle. Lead to guide others, help others, assist others. Lead so they may be successful. Lead so they may achieve greatness. Lead so they may rise above their own self-imposed limitations. Lead to serve their purposes and their desires. And in so doing, become an effective leader who serves based on your commitment to others.

That in itself is the greatest leader's understanding of capacity.

Self-Awareness: An awareness of one's own personality or individuality.

Leadership in Action: Self-awareness comes with experience, knowledge, observation, and participation. A willingness to learn from one's mistakes is critical to gaining a realistic understanding of who you are and how others see you. It can be a disarming journey for some, who unfortunately never quite get the handle on this leadership characteristic.

Becoming self-aware can be compared to learning to swim. It doesn't happen overnight, may take some fear to overcome, requires a good teacher, and requires consistent practice. It doesn't work to take a giant leap into the deep end. Although there are several people I know who could certainly use a big push in this direction.

LESSON #19: SERVE TO INSPIRE

A leader must inspire, or his team will expire.
—Orrin Woodward

If your actions inspire others to dream more, learn more, do more, and become more, you are a leader.
—John Quincy Adams

Being inspired, much like being motivated, is a unique and individual experience. What some may find motivating others may simply ignore. What inspires a person to act, to achieve, or to change a behavior can really only be understood via that individual person's reaction to an inspiring stimulus. Yet there are countless people whose stories, circumstances, and leadership characteristics are generally accepted as inspirational.

It is fact that many people find inspiration in their chosen religion and will use their spiritual beliefs to gain mental and emotional strength. Others may use science and education as a principle for living their lives and are inspired to do so in their principled beliefs. Many people look to their parents, siblings, family members, friends, and coworkers as models of inspiration. Those people who have a positive influence on their lives and provide a better and deeper understanding of support and help at all times, not just when it is needed most. Still others look to historical figures for words of wisdom and encouragement to help guide a positive attitude, change a behavior, or create a new degree of enlightenment.

A few examples of inspirational leaders include people like Nelson Mandela, the South African politician who led a life-long battle against apartheid in his country; Mahatma Gandhi, the antiwar activist whose words of peace and wisdom inspired millions as a leader of India's independence movement; Eleanor Roosevelt, the not so silent first lady to President Franklin Delano Roosevelt, who ofttimes challenged her husband's thinking and direction to inspire a nation with particular candidness and support for America's women.

Celebrities and entrepreneurs like Oprah Winfrey and J. K. Rowling endured personal challenges and hardships yet persevered and overcame their difficulties to inspire millions of people throughout the world with their personae and books.

Those people and their stories are well recognized and larger than life in status and achievement, and their impact on others is well documented. There are numerous others of celebrity who could be listed here. Conversely, there are many lesser-known leaders whose inspirational stories and actions would not be as recognizable. But those stories and actions would be recognized as equally impactful and effective by the individuals who were inspired by these lesser-known individuals.

As a sales training manager for 3M years ago, I would tell my training class attendees the story about one of those lesser-known inspirational leaders by the name of Glenn Cunningham. Ring a bell? I didn't think so. I will summarize the story briefly. Final sports analogy.

At the age of eight, Glenn Cunningham experienced a horrific tragedy that almost cost him his legs. He was severely burned in a schoolhouse fire, and Glenn's doctors recommended amputation as the only means of relief from his agony. Glenn was so distraught by the possibility of losing his legs that he begged his parents not to allow the procedure. The doctors feared the possibility of infection if Glenn's legs weren't amputated, an infection that could possibly lead to death. But Glenn's parents acquiesced to their son's pleas and canceled the surgery.

What happened over the next few years of recovery was nothing short of a miracle. Although scarred for life and having undergone countless hours of therapy, massage, and application of therapeutic ointment, Glenn regained the use of his legs. In fact he was not only determined to regain his ability to walk but also made a commitment to prove a point about his second chance to use his legs to their full capability.

Glenn healed in time and began to run, and not just to run for exercise. Glenn ran with intensity to compete. As a twelve-year-old, he regularly competed and won races against high school students. His passion for running, the appreciation granted to him by regaining the use of his legs, his practice and hard work led Glenn to set a Kansas state record in the mile. He later went on to record two NCAA titles and eight Amateur Athletic Association (AAU) titles at Kansas University. Those are certainly impressive accomplishments for a person who almost lost his legs.

But Glenn wasn't satisfied with what would be a well-ranked achievement for many others. Glenn competed in the 1932 and 1936 Olympics and earned a silver medal in the 1,500-meter run in 1936, setting a new US record. He then went on to earn his doctorate in biology, health, and physical education in 1940. He wrote a book entitled *Never Quit*,**** an autobiography that en-capsulates the entire inspirational story.

I have glossed here only a few paragraphs of a truly remark-able story that I highly recommend regardless of whether you have any interest whatsoever in athletics. Glenn's story is much more about the emotional and physical toll he was subjected to and his mental ability to overcome the odds stacked against him. His story of heroism and perseverance may be inspirational to those who can identify with hardship and physical challenges. It may also serve the same purpose for others who might not be dealing with a physical challenge but still need to be stimulated by a story of intense dedication and commitment to succeed. In short, the story is relatable on numerous levels.

**** Glenn Cunningham with George X. Sand, *Never Quit* (Chosen Books, 1981).

A leader needs to be relatable to inspire others. Being relatable is a foundation of successful leadership inspiration.

While inspiration comes to us in a variety of personal opportunities that we choose to accept or reject for our own reasons and beliefs, there are several characteristics common to all business leaders who are an inspiration to others in the workplace. The ability to inspire others is a skill set that many try to emulate, but is only effective for those who master and own their personal presence in these key areas.

- **Passion**—those who inspire are passionate about their subject matter and their ability to present their purpose. They are enthusiastic and positive in their approach and relentless in their emotional commitment to their interest. Their enthusiasm is contagious but never harmful to others because their belief is founded in doing good.

- **Integrity and trust**—those who inspire others operate with complete integrity at all times and are easily trusted because of their positive actions. They are committed to doing the right things and openly conduct their business in a manner that is appreciated and admired by their coworkers.

- **Value-driven**—inspirational leaders are value-driven. They visibly make a commitment to core values that are beneficial to their coworkers, customers, shareholders, and stakeholders. They are principled and focused on creating a worthwhile environment.

- **People-oriented**—inspirational leaders are invested in and committed to the personal development of their co-workers. They understand, acknowledge, and support the continuing education of their team with a commitment to improved learning environments that allows their co-workers to attain their full capacities.

- **Realistic**—those who inspire others are authentic in their approach, in their message, in their delivery, and in their belief. There is no room for flamboyance and arrogance. They are easily relatable and true to form so others are apt to engage and act.

- **Communicate**—inspirational leaders are skilled in their communications, understand their audience, deliver their message with passion and belief, and yet also speak in terms that coworkers will embrace and support. Their message is repeatable, confirmed, and enacted.

- **Unite others**—those who inspire have the ability to encourage unity and bring people together for a greater purpose. They do so with acceptance of all and tolerance for those who challenge, while staying strong to their intent. They are champions of diversity and inclusion. They clearly relate to the value of a strong team that emulates a diverse culture.

- **Fearless**—those who inspire are willing to be accountable for taking a risk, they own the results and are realistic in their desire to succeed while influencing others to take an empowered approach to their own personal success. They set the tone for others to believe in themselves and are examples of controlled confidence. Their courage is evident.

- **Human**—those who inspire always keep it real with a sense of humility and self-awareness. Their message is never above their own skill set, and their egos never get in the way of their desire to inspire others to be the best they can be.

- **Model**—inspirational leaders model their behavior and emulate their inspirational message. They live their belief, own their outcomes, and are consistent in their demonstration of their example. They are admired for who they are as much as for what they have to say.

As you are reading this lesson learned, I would venture that you may be thinking about or have already thought about someone in your life who inspired you. Maybe that person is currently in your life and continues to inspire you every day. Maybe that person has passed away, but their inspirational message continues on with you and will remain with you for the rest of your life. Hopefully, you will pass that inspiration down to others, perhaps in a way similar to the one in which it was delivered to you. Maybe you are in a situation wherein you need some inspiration, you need a person or event, or a reading or listening opportunity to get you to act, to feel better about yourself, your situation, your job or lack thereof, or your life in general.

My encouragement to you is to seek inspiration to be inspired yourself and to set the example for others to be inspired. Always look for the positive in life, which will guide you to improve your relationship, improve your work performance, or help you with your attitude. Continue to seek knowledge and associate yourself with others who are lifelong learners so you can continuously improve and develop. And most importantly, look for opportunities to be inspired to feel good about yourself so you will exude that same feeling to those with whom you share your life. They will appreciate your outlook, and your actions will have a positive influence on their approach to life.

> **Inspiration:** The process of being mentally stimulated to do or feel something, especially to do something creative.

> **Leadership in Action:** "The greatest inspiration comes to us from our own life experiences." I inscribed those words on numerous title pages of my first book with the intent to provide some inspiration to others to live and experience life to its fullest.

Being inspired is a little like being motivated. All it takes is one good life lesson learned to recognize the stimulus required to get something done. The best part about life in general is you get to choose from where your inspiration originates.

Choose with courage, faith, and conviction. But above all, choose with love.

LESSON #20: GET INVOLVED AND ACT

No involvement means no commitment—no exceptions.
—Dr. Laurie Buchanan

I regret that I never served in the US military. While of course it is best to go through life without regrets, I have several. Not serving in the military is one I think of often. I believe that service to one's country is one of the highest callings. Yet joining the military wasn't in my plan after high school. Back in the early seventies, it just wasn't "cool" to be militarized based on what had occurred in Vietnam and the protests here at home, which left a negative mindset on an impressionable seventeen-year-old. Yes, I graduated high school at seventeen and college at twenty-one. Not sure if that's relevant, except for the fact I really wasn't making any big career choice decisions at seventeen, and not many more a few years later at twenty-one.

Yet many people I met and had the pleasure of working with throughout my years told me on numerous occasions how I would have been perfect for the military. Many times I heard, "Ted, you would have enjoyed the military."

Now perhaps they meant that in a complimentary way based on my sense of commitment, organization, discipline, or my leadership style, or maybe it was just the military-style haircut that I have come to appreciate later in life. Perhaps they were referring to my exaggerated ability to be task-oriented or my type A, order-giving personality style. Maybe it was because they could relate my management style to their own personal military experience and that brought back some unforgettable memories. Perhaps mostly unpleasant unforgettable memories.

Yet regardless of my lack of military experience, I have always had a fascination with military leadership fueled by my fondness for history, specifically the American Civil War and World War II. I emulated the military generals who strategized and executed their plans during the course of battle. On a visit to Gettysburg National Military Park in Gettysburg, Pennsylvania, I was mesmerized by the landscape and its historical significance. I envisioned what had been. I was totally absorbed in the moment, the feeling of grief for lives lost, and the chills experienced when gazing out over the battlefield. What went through the minds of the leaders of that time can only be speculation on my part, yet to stand on that ground provided me with a sense of understanding of what I would have done had I been in command those days in July 1863.

Yet I am only a casual observer of the actual principles of military leadership. Certainly, there are volumes written on this subject, many by those who were experts in these strategic roles. My understanding of military leadership is based on reading history and in having to rely on others to tell me how much I would have enjoyed the military and its leadership style.

One of those people is a gentleman by the name of Wayne Brantley. In my opinion, Wayne is an expert in his chosen field of training and education and based on his military experience, is a highly credible source for exposition of the value of military leadership and lessons learned.

Wayne is currently the president of 360° Training Solutions based in Tampa, Florida. I met Wayne in 2012 and had the pleasure of working with him at Bisk Education for just about five years. In his role at Bisk as an associate vice president of professional education, Wayne served in a variety of teaching and training positions both internally and externally. Whether it was educating the newly hired enrollment representative class about the principles of project management or conducting an online college level course in the same subject matter or doing on-site training sessions for corporate clients like R. J. Reynolds, Lockheed-Martin, Boeing, Verizon, or Federal Express, Wayne was always involved in teaching, training, and educating others with the intent of helping them to improve their educational status. And not only was Wayne great in this role, but he also thoroughly enjoyed his responsibility to help others and still does so in his current role. By nature, he's a teacher, which in itself is an extraordinarily strong characteristic of a leader.

Wayne is what I would consider a lifelong learner. as evidenced by the accreditations he's earned, which follow his name. The list is long and impressive:

MsEd: Master of Education

PMP: project management professional

PMI-ACP: Project Management Institute agile certified practitioner

A-CSM: advanced certified scrum master

A-CSPO: advanced certified product owner

TKP: Team Kanban practitioner

ITIL: information technology information librarian

CPTD: certified professional in training and development

CRP: certified return-on-investment practitioner

PROSCI: certified change management practitioner

Certified John C. Maxwell Speaker, Trainer, and Coach

That is a credible and well-earned list of accreditations.

Yet regardless of what Wayne accomplished throughout his career, it's what happened to him early in his life that is of significant importance to the subject matter of this book and specifically this lesson learned.

At the young age of nineteen, Wayne enlisted in the US Air Force. He did so with the encouragement of his half-brother Leroy Natale, seventeen years his elder, who was an air force veteran. Wayne wanted to emulate his brother's experience and possibly to build his confidence and get a better direction for his own life. And in this vein, Wayne asked his brother Leroy for some advice before leaving for basic training.

Leroy gave Wayne this advice: *"Don't stick out, don't volunteer, and most important of all, you don't want to be the dorm chief."* Wayne would later find out the dorm chief is the guy who the training instructor (TI) places in charge of the flight of men, forty-nine others to be exact, when the TI is not around. This role and responsibility, as one would imagine, could bring about a severe baptism-by-fire learning opportunity for a nineteen-year-old who is trying to build his confidence, let alone get a sense of direction in life. And being dorm chief most certainly brings with it the potential to disengage the admiration, camaraderie, and friendliness of the other people in the flight. In fact being the dorm chief can be perceived as the extension of the TI, and not in a complimentary way. The dorm chief is the antagonist, the disciplinarian, the law, the authority, and ultimately if not respected by the others in the flight, the enemy.

From what I understand, the dorm chief is selected by the TI in one of two ways. To be considered, you have to be either the smallest person in the flight or the largest person in the flight. There is no other specific criterion. There is no dorm chief training manual. There is no prequalification testing. There is no job description or interview. There is no complicated selection process. There is a TI and the TI's choice.

At this time in his life Wayne was a strapping, six-one, well-chiseled body builder. He stood out from others simply because of his physique. So much so that when the TI, who stood a mere five-seven, first addressed Wayne, he called Wayne "Hulk," saying "You're damn big." This of course led to Wayne being assigned the role of temporary dorm chief. The word temporary signaled the intent of the TI to test Wayne, when in actuality it would be the other men in the flight who would end up testing Wayne throughout his term. The opportunity for harassment, dislike, and disdain notwithstanding, the mental strain placed on the dorm chief would surely be a significant challenge to the psyche of a still developing young man.

What a situation to be placed in. Here's Wayne assuming a leadership role with no leadership training or experience and no strategic support or direction while being asked to be responsible for the actions of forty-nine other people in a difficult and challenging six weeks of basic training.

From my perspective, the test is obvious, the assignment difficult, the learning experience unprecedented, and the results dependent upon the mental agility of the person placed into the challenge.

Wayne told me of a specific test that his flight underwent that was designed to measure and observe response and reaction and gauge how well the dorm chief interacted with the other people in the flight when faced with a crisis. During a routine training, senior military types entered the training facility and ordered the flight to assemble. Once they were organized, the senior military leaders told the flight that all training was being canceled and that they were to be immediately transported to Beirut, Lebanon. There they would support military personnel who were engaged in handling hostage situations. More mind games. More tests. More challenges. Yet some of the people in the flight were so totally sold and so believed the message was true that they began to cry. Can you imagine? What a shock. Here you are in basic training, learning the military way, taking classes in air traffic control, radar maintenance, computer training, and other technology platforms that have a direct civilian application designed to prepare you for a job once you leave the military, and now you are being told you will drop everything and go to one of the most volatile places on earth at that time. What's your reaction?

Wayne was fortunate to see through the charade fairly quickly. He realized this was just a test, and while it potentially could happen, it was designed to challenge and disrupt the status quo. Wayne handled it appropriately; he didn't panic. Others did. He was the one who had to engage his counterparts and encourage confidence, understanding, and empathy. He was, without actually knowing it, experiencing his first leadership moment.

While I question the tactics used by the senior military leaders in the brief example mentioned, I asked Wayne how that made him feel. Did he feel lied to? Aren't leaders supposed to be beacons of truth? Did he feel used?

On the contrary, Wayne viewed this situation as the eye-opening learning experience he had signed up for in the first place. He had been hoping to get a sense of direction from his military engagement, and this situation provided him with an ah-ha moment. He didn't panic when told of the "drop everything" message. He handled it. But best of all, he helped those around him handle it as well. And the light bulb went off—*he knew then and there that helping others through a moment of emergency or crisis is a foundation of leadership.* Perhaps he didn't know what to call it then and there, but he recognized that he had it within him.

Had Wayne not been selected dorm chief and been thrown into the first leadership test of his life, he may not have been enlightened about his love of learning and teaching and leading others via education. Maybe it would have happened later in life, but Wayne was fortunate to learn this about himself at such an early time in his life.

From that critical point and going forward, Wayne committed to the US Air Force's core values and became a champion for integrity, service before self, and excellence in all you do. He exemplified leadership at an early age and managed to guide others while learning how important the air force core values are to effective leadership.

Wayne earned the air force rank of master sergeant and was the superintendent of faculty development when he left the air force after seventeen years to pursue civilian life. At the time there were nearly one thousand instructors in his stead assigned to Keeler Air Force Base, trainers and teachers engaged in helping others to improve and better themselves through education. Wayne spent another seven years in the air force reserves volunteering when called upon to guide, teach, and lead through educating others.

And all because he was told not to be the dorm chief, or at least not to stand out so as not to be selected as the dorm chief. Nothing against Leroy.

Leaders understand the concept of getting involved, and they act accordingly. They are the ones who actively engage in problem-solving, solution offering, strategy building, and most importantly are the ones encouraging and helping others to achieve. Leaders are educators, teachers, trainers, instructors, and people who provide guidance to others. Simply stated, leaders get involved and act. Whether by choice or by selection, as in Wayne's case, leaders accept responsibility and are eager to encourage others to succeed.

Yet getting involved is only part of the equation. Knowing when and how to respond to a situation that requires action is critical to the leader's success. Equally important to recognizing and identifying a response-required situation is the leader's ability to think quickly and subsequently implement direction that is critical to not only the leader's success but also to the success and perhaps well-being of others involved in the scenario. People look to leaders for direction, support, answers, guidance and have an expectation that the leader will be the person who provides satisfactory fulfillment of their needs.

Regarding expectations, leaders do not hesitate. Leaders do not wait for a crisis to occur. Leaders avoid crisis by being proactive. Leaders ask questions, listen, learn, and act. Leaders make the necessary commitment to take responsibility. Leaders let their actions influence and drive desired results.

Most importantly, *leaders get involved*, make a commitment, and enjoy being at the core of responsibility.

Commitment: An agreement or pledge to do something in the future; the state or an instance of being obligated.

Leadership in Action: Commitment to solve a problem is something all great leaders know will either elevate them to a higher level of gratification once engaged or cause them to sink to a new level of learning, depending on the outcome of the solution to which they are committed.

Either way they win.

LESSON #21: ON THE WAY TO BECOMING A GREAT LEADER, BE A GREAT MANAGER AS WELL

Managers light a fire under people.
Leaders light a fire in people.
—Kathy Austin

Much is written regarding the difference between management and leadership and each of their practical applications in business. While the emphasis of this book is leadership in action, I want to use this final lesson learned to expound on the relationship between management and leadership. The two terms are intertwined, and while different in purpose, management and leadership are complementary to each other and must work together to ensure an organization's success. More importantly, management and leadership must be on the same page when it comes to respect and treatment of people. Again, without great people, there is no great organization. Better said, the foundation of all great organizations is built upon great people.

With that premise in mind, both management and leadership should have a common goal to work together to develop the organization's people. How they go about this assignment may differ, yet the concept must be ingrained in each role's responsibility in order to create a culture of appreciation for performance.

Investing in people to deliver expected results is common to both management and leadership, and its importance is paramount to an organization's success.

Yet as both entities engage in this prime assignment, at times the expectation placed on managers to immediately assume the role of a leader is misdirected. This is especially true for people newly promoted to a managerial role. These people performed well in their prior job and are selected or chosen to be considered for a supervisory position. Congratulations on your promotion—you earned the opportunity to assume more responsibility. While you understand the function of your prior job and are great at task completion, you now must learn how to supervise others, how to *manage*.

In that regard, many organizations will send a newly engaged supervisor/manager to a manager training session. It's a great opportunity to meet newly promoted counterparts and share in the learning experience. Along with providing information on the plethora of management responsibilities, these sessions also focus on a variety of managerial requirements from a

results-through-people point of view. Aiming to craft a successful manager, much of the training material covers topics that in
many cases are fresh ground for new supervisor/managers. Topics
such as communications, critical thinking / problem-solving,
customer interaction, employee performance discussions, time
management, teamwork, empathy, motivation, team building,
and decision-making are on the agenda for the newbie to absorb
and master. Sure—learn to be a manager-leader in a one-week
training session.

Not going to happen.

Many companies extend their training sessions to cover portions of these people skills by breaking up the sessions over the
course of several weeks, even months. The newbie can't be expected to learn everything in a single week, so many organizations take this approach: Let's provide smaller portions of important material over a larger amount of time to guide the new
manager so we allow them the opportunity to learn and actually
apply the key learnings while they are on the job. After all, we can
only prepare them to the extent of what they can absorb and put
to good use. We want them to be successful in their roles.

Well, that's a little better approach for sure. No sense drinking from the fire hose.

A third approach combines the classroom training with on-
the-job training under the supervision of a coach or mentor.
The new manager shadows the coach to watch and learn from
someone successful in the role. The coach is an experienced

manager-leader in his own right and spends time working with the new manager to assist and guide in situations that may be out of the norm of the daily tactical managerial routine. The new manager has access to a coach who oftentimes is a sounding board, mentor, confidant, and trusted adviser. Provided the coach has the best interests of the new manager in mind, and in the majority of cases they do, the new manager is on the right path to an enhanced managerial skill set.

While these three scenarios represent only a few of the available options for companies to assist new managers in becoming better managers, and while I support a focused effort by senior leaders to get involved in this regard, I believe the process to becoming a great manager takes time and effort and can't be accomplished without longevity of process and experience. How long a time and how much effort depends on the requirements and the complexity of the position, but generally managers don't become great managers overnight. Nor do great managers become great leaders in the blink of an eye.

Learning to be a great manager takes time, effort, and experience. Learning to be a great leader takes a proportionate amount of time, effort, and experience.

As groundwork to build on that critical statement, here's a basic list of role responsibilities / characteristics / areas of emphasis for both managers and leaders. My intent here is not to categorize and separate the two roles but rather to provide definitions of general terms of primary focus for each role. There is crossover depending on the individual situation and circumstances and especially application. Remember the part about these roles being intertwined and needing to be thus for optimal success in developing people? Yet I also want to offer these brief summary statements with the caveat that while they are simple in phrasing, their individual meanings and the subsequent actions required are much more complex in reality.

As an example, "managing by doing" certainly requires an ability to perform the required tasks assigned to the job in order to teach and assist others to perform the job (i.e., while perhaps this is not a daily duty, the grocery store manager certainly needs to know how to operate the cash register, understand the checkout process, be familiar with the scanning system, and know how to engage in corrective action should any of the systems falter.)

Similarly, the leader values the importance of influencing others to perform their duties in line with the overall company strategy yet realizes consistent actions require in-depth understanding of stimulus/motivation, encouragement, coaching, feedback, reward and recognition, and the ability to use these skill sets in the appropriate manner and at the appropriate time. Setting a positive example as a leader is much more complex in execution than it is in mere rhetoric.

In general:

Manager	Leader
Task-oriented	People-oriented
Manages by doing	Leads by influence
Coordinates workers	Develops people
Works for goal achievement	Creates organizational vision
Motivates as needed	Inspires incessantly
Builds systems	Builds relationships
Solves problems	Implements solutions
Thinks in the moment	Visualizes for the future
Communicates for process	Communicates for inspiration
Controls situations	Establishes trust
Stays in a system	Creates positive change
Risk-averse	Risk-taker
Directs employees	Builds followers

When you read the above characteristics, you most likely recognized that you are not set into just one side of the equation, that you are at times required to move back and forth depending on the situation and circumstances. This proves my point about the two roles being intertwined. Commonalities exist in practical application of the role responsibilities, just as they exist in the circumstances of the people in action in these roles.

For further clarification, have you ever worked with a manager who was spot-on in every task-oriented function of his role but was a bit lacking or severely lacking on the leadership side of the role? By the same token, have you been guided by a leader who was simply a marvel of vision and a tremendous change agent but didn't have a clue as to what the frontline workers in the organization actually did to make things work? My point is, neither one of those people is fully effective in their roles and perhaps is not interested in understanding or does not have the capacity to understand the importance of the crossover in their responsibilities. They categorize themselves unintentionally. They forgot or never knew what got them to where they are at. Or they just don't care. That's not great management—and certainly not great leadership.

As I mentioned previously, I am a firm believer that the requirement of time, experience, and effort is at the core of developing great leadership skills. However, I am also a firm believer that the person who puts in the time, effort, and learns from their experiences as a manager places himself in a much better position to learn to be a great leader.

In essence, *on the way to becoming a great leader, be a great manager as well.*

Those who master the art of management and use that as a foundation for implementing great leadership stand a much better chance of being successful in their roles. They understand the importance of the *knowledge of doing* as a prerequisite to leading.

Mastering the art of management requires personal knowledge of how things work in the organization. Mastering the art of leadership requires knowing how those things work and what effect they have in relation to the organization's people. Do you see the connection?

Too often people are thrust into managerial roles and are expected to be leaders at the same time. Too often they fail because they are not fully prepared to assume the complex responsibilities of their roles. They have yet to learn the importance of management in their quest to lead. They have yet to fully engage themselves in the left-hand-column duties, responsibilities, and characteristics in order to prepare themselves for the right-hand-column level of complexity.

If you are ever doubting yourself as to the importance of your management responsibilities during your quest to learn and become a great leader, just think of these simple scenarios as they may assist in your thinking.

When customers in a retail environment want to lodge a complaint, they ask for *the manager*.

When diners at a restaurant have an issue with a meal, they ask for *the manager*.

When callers aren't satisfied with their customer service, they ask for *the manager*.

It's not too often that people will ask for *the leader*. They know if they want an immediate answer to an issue, it's going to be *the manager* who will solve their problem.

That experience as a manager in handling customer's issues is paramount to understanding what is required to be positioned for success as a great leader. It is the knowledge and skill set of doing that provides the foundation for leaders to act, and simply stated, the majority of leaders are able to take appropriate action because they have gained enough experience as managers to be confident in their decision-making process.

I applaud those organizations that empower their frontline managers to make legitimate customer service, customer pleasing decisions without having to get approval from a next-level-up leader. Those organizations understand the importance of allowing these current managers and next generation leaders to feel great about their decisions at an early experience level. They know these investments will pay dividends for their future leaders as well as their current customers. They fully understand the influence they have on their manager's commitment to perform their jobs in exemplary fashion.

But more importantly these organizations who demonstrate that philosophy are led by people who enact the principle of leadership defined as leadership in action. They trust, empower, engage, develop, communicate, and invest in the people who are their organization. And they know why they need to execute this responsibility for their people to the utmost level of support.

After all, they were once managers, and their support as a leader is expected. There are no business guarantees that provide a straight and narrow path to becoming a great leader. Even if one succeeds at being a great manager, becoming a great leader is not guaranteed. The journey is complex, challenging, filled with obstacles and barriers, and at times unpredictable. Yet those that practice the art of management and keep a commitment to their people throughout their learning experience will always have a better foundation on which to build their leadership skills. People will recognize the manager-leader who places their best interests in mind, has their back, works for their development, supports their personal and professional goals, and places himself in a servant leadership position as a manager-leader who is on the path to becoming a great leader. They recognize this is more than a boss-employee transactional relationship. They recognize a true partnership with a manager-leader who cares about them and their responsibility to the organization.

Is there a secret sauce to great leadership? Hardly. Great leadership is one of those intangible phrases that comes with time, effort, experience, and a ton of positive reinforcement. Great leadership is hard to describe outside a plethora of complimentary terms but easily recognizable when seen in action. While plenty of words are offered to describe what great leadership is, the only true measure of great leadership is to actually see it in action. Great leaders are great leaders based on their actions and the effects those actions have on their constituents. Many have the ability to understand and share in another's feelings, which defines empathy, yet it's the actions of the person based on this understanding that define true leadership.

Resourcefulness: Able to meet situations; capable of devising ways and means

Leadership in Action: It is said that great managers don't need to have all the answers; they just need to be resourceful enough to know how and where to find the right answers. The same can be said about great leaders.

When great leaders need to know the right answers, they just need to be resourceful enough to know where to look for those great managers.

BONUS LESSON LEARNED
SEVERAL GUIDING LEADERSHIP
IN ACTION PRINCIPLES

- *Lead by acknowledging people, and approach every day with a sense of humility in your encounters.*
- *Lead by building a team that emulates your leadership core values of trust, integrity, and honesty.*
- *Lead by being an active listener; pay close attention to those in your stead to provide encouragement and support when needed.*
- *Lead by being a champion of individual problem-solving, and in so doing empower others to think and act with independent creative reason.*
- *Lead by having an exceptional work ethic; let no one in the organization question your dedication and commitment to the effort at hand.*
- *Lead by being a lifelong learner, and share your desire to learn openly without hesitation or fear of rebuttal.*
- *Lead by building a team of unique and diverse individuals that complement each other's skill set.*

- *Lead by doing the right things right; recognize and reward others for leading in the same manner.*
- *Lead by owning your results and by being accountable for either the success or failure of your strategy.*
- *Lead by having a plan B, but work the hell out of plan A first.*

Intelligence: The ability to learn or understand or to deal with new or trying situations; the skilled use of reason.

Leadership in Action: True leaders have a complete understanding of what it means to be intelligent. They've learned the best way to demonstrate this understanding is to hire people smarter than themselves and empower them to do their jobs.

In other words, get out of their way, and let them do their jobs.

Definitions sourced from *Merriam-Webster*, https://www.merriam-webster.com/dictionary.